A Practical Guide to Pensions and Life Insurance

A Practical Guide to Pensions and Life Insurance

Simon Shirley, FCA

CHARTERED
ACCOUNTANTS
IRELAND

Published in 2020 by
Chartered Accountants Ireland
Chartered Accountants House, 47 Pearse Street, Dublin 2
The Linenhall, 32-38 Linenhall Street, Belfast BT2 8BG
www.charteredaccountants.ie

ISBN: 978-1-912350-95-7

Typeset by Datapage
Printed and bound by CPI Group (UK) Ltd, Croydon, CR0 4YY

MIX
Paper from
responsible sources
FSC   FSC® C013604
www.fsc.org

Introduction

For many of us, a pension plan will be one of our most important financial assets at retirement. Pensions exist so we can afford to stop working one day, and many of us will retire several years before we are due to receive the state pension, which in any case may not be enough to provide us with a financially flexible retirement. The state pension in its current form may not even be sustainable in the decades to come; therefore, relying only on it to provide our income in retirement may not be wise.

Life insurance protection for us and our families in the event of serious illness or death is another key element of our personal financial planning.

Even if we understand the importance of pensions, *prioritising* pension planning can be challenging. While we understand that we need to take action during our working lives to be able to afford to stop working at some point, our short- and medium-term needs often take precedence over making provision for the future. Action that leads to short-term rather than long-term results can be more attractive, leading us to postpone long-term financial planning, or put it 'on the long finger'.

For many, appropriate pension and life insurance planning options will also depend on how our personal lives and work lives develop and change over time. **Figure 0.1** on the following page depicts an indicative financial path through life and highlights some of the financial planning stages that we may encounter along the way. The path begins with starting work (in our late teens/early 20s for many of us) and ends when we are in retirement. Along the way, the various stages include buying a house, starting a family, saving and investing, and planning for retirement. These stages are annotated in the figure with the elements of pension and life insurance planning that we will need to consider along the way and as discussed in this book.

Although the basic concept of pension planning is straightforward and makes sense – putting money aside during our working lives for our retirement – successfully navigating through the wide range of options, benefits and restrictions can be difficult and complex. Terms like 'investment risk', 'volatility profile', 'cash and cash equivalents', 'tax allowable contributions' and 'net relevant earnings' can confuse many people and often induce the 'glaze' that all pension advisors recognise!

FIGURE 0.1: THE FINANCIAL PATH THROUGH LIFE

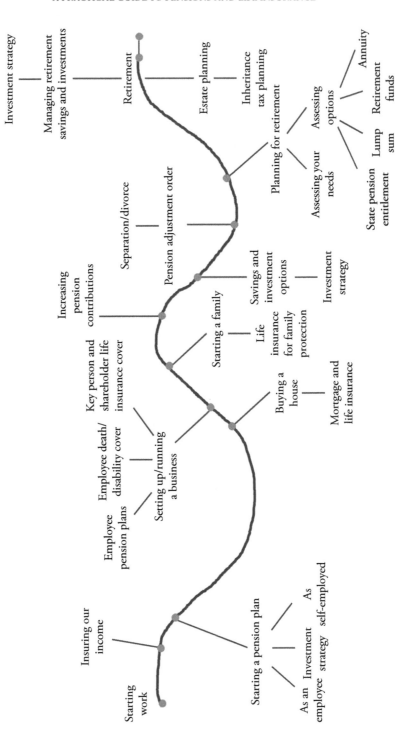

Over 50% of the Irish workforce do not have a personal or employer-offered pension plan, and many workers who do have a pension plan in place are not saving enough for their retirement, meaning that they will need to work for longer and/or will struggle financially when they do retire.

This book demonstrates the benefits of saving for a pension, including significant support from the State, which effectively contributes up to €2 for every €3 paid into pensions, in the form of tax relief. The pensions landscape is changing, with a number of major developments and changes underway, including the proposed introduction of 'automatic enrolment' by 2022, proposed changes to tax relief on pension contributions, and increased governance and supervision for pension plans at an EU-wide level. The more you know, the better positioned you will be to take advantage of pensions for your personal benefit and, in the case of advisors, for the benefit of your clients.

Accountants, tax advisors and other financial advisors who provide financial planning advice to individuals and businesses should have a clear understanding of the basics of pension planning, life insurance protection, and the tax reliefs available. This book is a practical, easy-to-follow guide, backed up by appropriate technical information, providing relevant information clearly and concisely to assist you in making informed decisions or in advising others to make informed decisions.

While this book makes reference to defined benefit (DB) pension plans (i.e. pension plans that 'promise to pay' retirement benefits to employees, typically on the basis of salary and years of service), it focuses mainly on defined contribution (DC) pension plans, which provide retirement benefits on the basis of on an accumulated savings value. Defined contribution plans are the most common type of pension plan available to and used by employees in small and medium-sized businesses, self-employed individuals and business owners.

Outline of this Book

The seven chapters of this book are summarised as follows:

- **Chapter 1: Pension Planning** An overview of pension planning, this chapter summarises the various pension plan structures available and introduces a number of key elements of pension planning, including tax relief on contributions, taking benefits from pension plans, pension plan costs, rules and regulations. This chapter also discusses the demographic challenges facing the state pension system and recent developments in the Irish pension landscape.

- **Chapter 2: Investment Assets and Strategies** This chapter covers the typical investments held in pension plans and the types of investment strategies undertaken, levels of risk and volatility, and the importance of diversification.
- **Chapter 3: Pension Planning for Sole Traders, Partners and Company Owners** The range of pension plan options available to self-employed business owners are examined in this chapter, including PRSAs, personal pension plans and occupational pension schemes. Revenue maximum contribution levels and Revenue maximum funding calculations are explained, along with self-administered pension plan structures.
- **Chapter 4: Employee Pension and Life Insurance Plans** This chapter discusses the pension plan options typically provided by employers for employees, i.e. through group occupational pension schemes and group PRSAs. Additional voluntary contributions (AVCs) by employees, options for employee pension plans when leaving employment and group employee life insurance plans providing benefits in the event of death or disability are also covered.
- **Chapter 5: Life Insurance for Individuals and Businesses** The main types of life insurance (in addition to group life insurance cover for employees as covered in **Chapter 4**) are discussed in this chapter, including cover for death and illness. Typical costs for life insurance are provided, as well as the personal tax reliefs available. Life insurance options for businesses are also discussed, including key person cover and shareholder cover.
- **Chapter 6: Planning for Retirement** This chapter looks at the various options for taking retirement benefits from pension plans, including lump sums, annuities and retirements funds, and describes what happens to pension plans on death and discusses 'early' retirement options.
- **Chapter 7: Separation and Divorce** An overview of pension plan benefits in the context of separation and divorce, including pension adjustment orders, are discussed in this chapter.

Acknowledgements

I wish to thank the following:

- Chartered Accountants Ireland, and in particular Michael Diviney, who suggested this book a number of years ago and expertly guided me through the publishing process;
- John Killeen of New Ireland Assurance and John McInerney of Aviva, who provided indispensable technical editing of the text during its draft stages;
- my colleagues, who continually go the extra mile in assisting and supporting me and our clients;
- our firm's chairperson, Anthuan Xavier, who has provided invaluable support, friendship and counsel over the last 20+ years; and
- my family, who encouraged me over the hurdles and past the finishing line.

1.
Pension Planning

Introduction

The concept of pension planning is straightforward: we put some of our earnings aside during our working lives so that we have savings to provide for our retirement. However, in practice, many of us underestimate the level of savings required to provide an adequate income in retirement, or we do not take full advantage of the benefits available from tax-efficient pension structures.

Pension planning is one of three key objectives of long-term financial planning. By retirement age (typically between age 60 and 70) we should aim to:

1. have an adequate level of pension income;
2. be debt free; and
3. have accessible savings and/or investments.

FIGURE 1.1: THREE KEY LONG-TERM FINANCIAL OBJECTIVES

Objective 1: Pension income	Objective 2: Debt	Objective 3: Savings/investments
To have an adequate level of pension income	To be debt free	To have accessible savings and/or investments

The following topics covered in this chapter provide an overview of the key features of pension planning:

- challenges to state pensions;
- what is a 'pension plan'?
- state incentives for pension plans;
- investing a pension plan;
- when to start and how to save;
- tax relief on pension contributions;
- employer contributions;
- pension plan and retirement plan structures;

- benefits from a pension plan;
- typical costs of a pension plan;
- rules and regulations;
- developments in the pensions landscape.

Challenges to State Pensions

The state pension system in many countries, whereby the state provides a pension to citizens in retirement, is the main source of retirement income for many individuals. However, state pension systems in their current form may not be sustainable in decades to come. This is due to several reasons, including the ageing population in many countries and the fact that people are living longer, which is resulting in increasing costs to the State in providing pensions that may ultimately become unaffordable.

As a result, significant developments and changes are likely to occur in the pensions landscape in the coming years, including the automatic enrolment of workers in a pension plan (discussed further below).

'Promise to pay' pension systems exist in many European countries, whereby the State commits or 'promises to pay' a pension to citizens based on a range of criteria, such as earnings levels, length of time in the workforce, etc. Ireland operates such a system and mainly relies on the existing workforce to pay for the pensions of older, retired citizens.

At the time of writing, the maximum State Pension (Contributory) amount payable by the Irish State is €248.30 per week and qualifying age for receiving this pension is 66.

Entitlement to the State Pension (Contributory) is not means-tested and is based on the number of PRSI contributions paid by an individual. Individuals who do not qualify for the State Pension (Contributory), or only qualify for a reduced amount, may be entitled to the State Pension (Non-Contributory). The entitlement to the State Pension (Non-Contributory) is means-tested. (See www.citizensinformation.ie for more information – a detailed commentary and analysis of the State pension system is beyond the scope of this book.)

As mentioned above, this system is unlikely to be sustainable in Ireland in its current form because the proportion of the population in retirement is steadily increasing and the proportion of the population in work is reducing. Over time, this is likely to result in an increasing percentage of the State's resources being spent on healthcare and pensions for older people, with potentially insufficient tax revenue coming in from the working population to support these spending increases.

In its *2018 Ageing Report*,[1] the Department of Finance included the following stark projections reflecting the 'Great Demographic Shift' in Ireland.

"Ireland's demographic profile is set to change significantly over the forecast period [2016–2070 period]. The share of the population aged 65 and over is set to nearly double from 13.4% in 2016 to a peak of 25.9% in 2054 before falling slightly to 24.2% in 2070.

In contrast, the share of the working age population (WAP defined for these purposes as those aged 20-64) is projected to gradually decline during the period, from approximately 58% in 2016 to 51% in 2050. Reflecting these changes, the old age dependency ratio is set to increase from approximately 21% in 2016 to a peak of 46% in 2053 before falling to 41% by 2070.

Such shifts in Ireland's demographic profile would have significant implications for the evolution of the public finances. Foremost amongst these is a substantial rise in age-related public expenditure as a larger share of the population move into age brackets requiring such spending."

The 'old age dependency ratio' is defined as the population aged 65+ divided by the population aged 15-64 (i.e. "the working age population").

The projections above highlight that:

At present, we have 5 workers (aged 15-64) for every 1 senior citizen (aged 65+).

By 2050, we will have 2 workers for every 1 senior citizen.

Therefore, relying only on the State to provide for our retirement may not be an option for many of us in decades to come. We will need to rely on our own private pension plans, savings and investments to provide us with an adequate level of income in retirement.

[1] *2018 Ageing Report: Ireland Country Fiche* (Department of Finance, 2018) https://ec.europa.eu/info/sites/info/files/economy-finance/final_country_fiche_ie.pdf

What is a 'Pension Plan'?

Accumulating sufficient savings in a tax-efficient manner during our working lives for retirement is an essential component of personal financial planning. Using a pension plan structure for this purpose is an efficient way of achieving this financial planning objective.

A pension plan is a tax-efficient savings and investment structure approved by the Revenue Commissioners (Revenue) to provide financial benefits to the plan holder during retirement, or to the plan holder's dependants in the event of their death. Benefits from pension plans are payable in addition to State pension entitlements.

- A pension is what you receive when you have retired, i.e. your income in retirement.

- A pension plan is the investment savings plan you pay into before you retire, building a fund to provide you with a pension when you do retire.

Pension plan products are offered by a range of financial services providers, such as life insurance companies, banks and stockbrokers, typically offering a wide range of low-, medium- and higher-risk funds, and access to direct investments, in which pension contributions can be invested.

State Incentives for Pension Plans

The State wants as many people as possible to have a pension income in retirement, and not to rely solely on the State for their retirement income. To encourage this, the State provides two important incentives in the form of tax relief for individuals:

1. **Growth earned on investments in pension plans is not subject to tax in Ireland.** In simple terms: you pay into a pension plan in the expectation that the plan will grow over time and earn money. Tax is typically payable on investment earnings/growth; however, the State does not tax such earnings/growth in pension plans.
2. **Tax relief is provided on payments you make into your pension plan (subject to limits).** In simple terms: you do not pay income

tax/PAYE on whatever proportion of your income that you chose to pay into a pension plan (subject to limits, as discussed later in this chapter). This tax relief means that if you make a pension contribution of €5, you receive tax relief of up to €2 (for higher-rate taxpayers (40%)), resulting in a net cost to you of €3 after tax.

At present, for every €3 of your cash that you pay into your pension plan, the State effectively pays in up to €2.

Accessing the Funds in a Pension Plan

As a 'quid-pro-quo' for benefiting from these generous tax reliefs, the State restricts access to the savings in a pension plan until we are aged 60 or upwards (although there are some important exceptions, as discussed later in this book). These restrictions help to ensure that we do not spend the money in our pension plans during our working lives, i.e. this money generally should only be used to provide us with an income in retirement, not beforehand.

Pension plan savings are typically accessed on retirement by withdrawing a lump sum, some or all of which may be tax-free, and using the balance to provide a regular income during retirement. (See **Chapter 6** for more information.)

Investing a Pension Plan

During your working life, your pension plan will be invested in order to grow its value. A key objective during the savings period, therefore, is to invest the pension plan so that the growth in the plan can match or exceed inflation in the long term. Investment managers of pension plans invest in 'growth assets,' such as company shares and property for this purpose. A pension plan will typically provide a number of investment options that an individual can select, depending on their preferences and tolerance for investment risk and volatility. (See **Chapter 2** for information on investments in pension plans.)

The value of a pension plan is typically made up of three key components, as shown in **Figure 1.2** below.

FIGURE 1.2: KEY COMPONENTS OF A PENSION PLAN

* Investments can fall as well as rise in value.

The 'tax saving paid in' is another way of looking at the tax relief; for example, a pension contribution of €100 would result in a tax saving of up to €40 (up to 40% income tax/PAYE saving). Therefore, the net cost would be €60, i.e. the pension contribution of €100 paid in is made up of 'your cash' of €60 + the 'tax saving' of €40.

The 'investment growth' is the income and gains that the investments held in the pension plan may generate over time, for example, dividends on shares held by the pension plan, the increase in the value of the shares, etc. (see **Chapter 2** for more detail).

If you are an employee and your employer also pays a contribution into your pension plan, your plan value will typically be made up of four key components, as shown in **Figure 1.3** below.

FIGURE 1.3: KEY COMPONENTS OF AN EMPLOYER-PROVIDED PENSION PLAN

* Investments can fall as well as rise in value.

(Employer-provided pension plans are discussed in detail in **Chapter 4**.)

When to Start and How to Save

The earlier you begin saving, the more money you will have saved by retirement. Even saving small amounts at the beginning of a career can make a big difference at the end, and saving regularly is an important financial discipline. Irrespective of your age, if you have taxable earnings, then you should ensure that you benefit from making contributions to a Revenue-approved pension plan, due to the tax reliefs that are available.

In practice, many individuals start contributing to a pension plan in their mid to late 20s or early 30s and increase their level of contributions as their careers develop over time.

The 'Half-your-age Rule'

The 'half-your-age rule' is a general rule of thumb for how much someone should contribute to their pension plan. In order to provide a pension fund that is capable of providing at least 50% of your earnings in retirement, the percentage of your earnings paid into a pension plan should be half your age throughout your working life. For example, a 40-year old should make pension contributions of 20% of earnings, a 50-year old should make pension contributions of 25% of earnings, and so on. Employer contributions, if relevant, would count towards this target.

For many, this rule of thumb is only aspirational and may not be affordable due to other costs of living such as mortgage payments, childcare and education costs, etc. Personal financial circumstances will dictate the level of pension contributions that are affordable. The starting point is to assess the realistic and maintainable amount of net earnings that can be saved into a pension plan on an ongoing basis, i.e. the amount you can afford to save each month, each year, etc.

Saving a Quarter of Earnings

A simple way of appreciating the level of savings required for a financially secure retirement is to assume that many of us will work for 40 years or so, i.e. from our mid-20s to our mid-60s.

On the basis that we expect to live to our mid-80s, then our time in retirement will be **half** the time we spend working.

So, if you want to have an income in retirement (excluding any State pension that may be paid) that is half your earnings when working, then, in simple terms:

| half of your working life during retirement | × | half of your earnings required in retirement | = | a **quarter** of your earnings are required to be saved on average throughout your working life* |

* *Employer contributions, if relevant, would count towards this 'quarter of earnings' target.*

EXAMPLE 1.1: SAVING A QUARTER OF EARNINGS

If Maeve currently earns €60,000 and works for 40 years (say from age 25 to 65), and spends 20 years in retirement (from age 65 to 85), then the amount she will need to save each year can be calculated as follows:

$$\frac{20 \text{ years (retirement)}}{40 \text{ years (working)}} \times 50\% \text{ of earnings} = \frac{25\% \text{ of earnings}}{\text{to be saved each year}}$$

'Save More Tomorrow'

An alternative approach is 'save more tomorrow': if your after-tax earnings increase each year, say by 2–3%, increase your pension contributions by 1–2% each year. This approach can steadily increase pension contributions in a manageable way over time. A related approach is to aim to save a percentage of salary increases as a pension contribution:

"Each time my salary increases, I will save 25% of the increase by increasing my pension contributions."

EXAMPLE 1.2: USING SALARY INCREASES IN PENSION PLANNING

John's salary is €48,000. He is promoted and receives a salary raise of 10%, i.e. an increase of €4,800, or €400 per month.

John decides to save 25% of this raise by increasing his pension contribution by €100 per month (25% of €400).

The tax saving on the increased pension contribution of €100 is €40 (assuming John's higher PAYE rate is 40%: €100 × 40% = €40).

Therefore, John has effectively used €60 of the increase in his net salary to increase his pension contributions by €100 per month.

John's salary raise per month = €400	He decides to pay 25% of the raise to his pension plan = €100	PAYE tax saving at 40% of this contribution = €40	Net salary cost of the pension contribution (€100 less €40) = €60

Tax Relief on Pension Contributions

At the time of writing, annual income up to €35,300 is subject to income tax/PAYE at 20%, known as the 'standard rate', and this income band of €35,300 is known the 'standard rate tax band'. In the case of married couples/civil partners with **one income**, the standard rate tax band is increased to €44,300. Income above the standard rate tax band is subject to income tax/PAYE at 40%, which is known as the 'higher rate'. Income is also subject to PRSI (social insurance contributions) and USC (the Universal Social Charge, which is a tax payable on total income).

For employees, tax relief on pension contributions is granted by deducting the pension contribution amount from income before calculating the relevant income tax/PAYE rate (i.e. a rate of 20% or 40%). However, PRSI and USC must still be paid on the pension contribution amount, i.e. tax relief for PRSI or USC is not available

Therefore, if an individual's annual income exceeds the standard rate tax band, the tax relief on their pension contributions is calculated based on the individual's higher rate (40%), to the extent that the pension contributions do not exceed the amount of income taxed at the higher rate (see **Example 1.3** below).

EXAMPLE 1.3: HOW TAX RELIEF IS CALCULATED ON PENSION CONTRIBUTIONS

Mark has an annual salary of €36,000 and is taxed as a single person.

Income tax/PAYE on Mark's salary is as follows: €35,300 is subject to income tax/PAYE at 20% (the 'standard rate'); the balance of **€700** is taxed at 40% (the 'higher rate').

Mark makes a pension contribution of €100 per month, i.e. **€1,200** per year.

As Mark's annual pension contribution of €1,200 exceeds the balance of Mark's salary of €700 that is taxed at 40%, the tax relief on these pension contributions is calculated as follows:

€700 contribution × 40% higher rate + €500 contribution balance × 20% standard rate = €380 tax relief

If Mark's salary increases to €36,500 (or higher), tax relief at the 40% higher rate would apply to **all** of the €1,200 contribution, as follows:

€1,200 contribution × 40% higher rate = €480 tax relief

Limits apply to the tax relief that an individual can claim on their pension contributions. These limits consist of:

1. age-related percentage limits (see **Figure 1.4** below) that increase as we get older; and
2. an annual gross earnings limit of €115,000.

FIGURE 1.4: AGE-RELATED PERCENTAGE LIMITS FOR TAX RELIEF

Age	Contribution Limits for Tax Relief (% of remuneration/net relevant earnings)
Under 30	15%
30 to 39	20%
40 to 49	25%
50 to 54	30%
55 to 59	35%
60+	40%

For example, a 40-year old with earnings of €60,000 per annum can contribute up to 25% of their gross earnings to a pension plan for tax relief purposes, i.e. tax-allowable pension contributions of up to €15,000 per annum, or €1,250 per month. This individual would only pay income tax/PAYE on earnings of €45,000 (i.e. gross earnings of €60,000 less the €15,000 pension contribution).

For higher rate taxpayers, the tax relief is equivalent to an additional bonus contribution of 67% of the net contribution, i.e. every €100 contributed to a pension plan costs €60, net of tax relief, so the tax relief of €40 is effectively an additional contribution added to the net contribution of €60, i.e. 67% of the net contribution:

    €100 paid into a pension plan
    – €40 tax relief (i.e. 40% × €100 for higher rate taxpayers)
    = €60 net cost for the individual

The €40 tax relief equates to 67% of the €60 net cost. In other words, the €40 tax relief can be viewed as a 'bonus' on top of the €60 net cost to the individual.

EXAMPLE 1.4: 'BONUS' OF UP TO 67% OF NET COST OF PAYMENTS TO A PENSION PLAN

Kasia is aged 35 and is taxed as a single person. She earns a gross salary of €60,000 per year (€5,000 per month) and decides to pay 10% of her salary into a pension plan.

Kasia's pension contribution is €500 per month (i.e. 10% × €5,000). In other words, she is diverting €500 of her gross salary to the pension plan each month. As a result, Kasia will be subject to income tax/PAYE on salary of €4,500 per month, not on €5,000 per month.

Kasia's income tax on her salary is reduced by the tax saving on this pension contribution. The tax saving is 40%, therefore Kasia's income tax on salary is reduced by €200 (pension contribution of €500 × 40% = €200).

The actual cost of the pension contribution for Kasia is €300, as Kasia's net pay each month is reduced by €300 (not €500), even though €500 is paid into the pension plan.

Kasia has saved €500 for a cost of €300, i.e. Kasia has effectively received a 'bonus' of €200 on the net cost of €300. This 'bonus' of €200 equates to a bonus of 67% on the net cost to Kasia.

In other words, the cash cost to Kasia is €300, and the income tax of €200 that Kasia would otherwise have paid is effectively paid into the pension plan.

For every €3 Kasia contributes to her pension plan, the State effectively pays in up to €2 by not deducting income tax/PAYE from her gross salary that is paid in to her pension plan.

Note: the Irish Government has proposed the introduction of an automatic enrolment ('auto enrolment') system by 2022 as part of the 'Pensions Roadmap' (*A Roadmap for Pensions Reform 2018–2023* (Government of Ireland, 2018), with a suggested State contribution of €1 for every €3 paid in by employees, to replace existing tax relief. This proposal of €1 for every €3 would equate to flat tax relief of 25%, which would be more advantageous than the current tax relief for lower paid workers who receive tax relief at 20% on pension contributions at present, but less advantageous for higher paid workers who are currently benefiting from 40% tax relief in many cases. (The Pensions Roadmap is further discussed later in this chapter.)

Employer Contributions

Employers can also make contributions to employee pension plans. Employer pension contribution levels may not be subject to the limits shown in **Figure 1.4** above, depending on the type of pension plan. (See **Chapter 4** for more information on pension plans for employees.)

Employer contributions are often made on a 'minimum-matching' basis, i.e. the employee must at least match the employer contribution in order to benefit from it. (Employer contribution levels are discussed in detail in **Chapter 3**.)

At present, though employers are legally obliged to provide employees with access to a pension plan, employers are not obliged to make payments into the plan. However, employer contributions are likely to become mandatory if an auto-enrolment system is introduced (as per the 'Pensions Roadmap').

Employer pension contributions are allowable as a trading expense for business tax purposes. In addition, employer contributions (subject to limits) are not treated as a benefit-in-kind (BIK) for employees. This means that employees are not liable to income tax, PRSI or USC on those employer contributions. Furthermore, employer contributions to employee pension plans are **not** subject to employer PRSI.

EXAMPLE 1.5: EMPLOYER CONTRIBUTIONS

Mary is employed by XYZ Limited and has an annual salary of €50,000. Mary makes a pension contribution of 5% each month and XYZ Limited makes a matching pension contribution of 5%.

The net cost to Mary is €125 each month – the total amount paid into Mary's pension plan is €416 per month, as illustrated below:

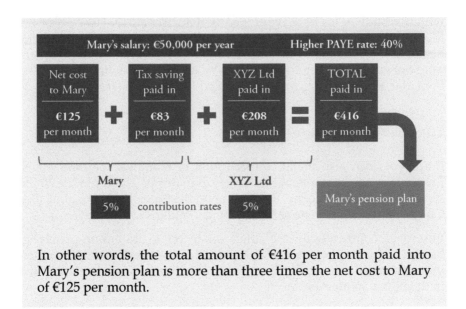

In other words, the total amount of €416 per month paid into Mary's pension plan is more than three times the net cost to Mary of €125 per month.

The combination of an employer contribution plus the tax relief on an employee's contributions results in a significant savings benefit for the employee. An employer contribution to a pension plan is a very valuable benefit for employees and is a strong incentive for employees to make their own pension contributions and to benefit from the tax relief. An employer pension contribution is often a key component in an employee benefits package to help employers attract and retain employees (see the "Examples of Employee Pension Plan and Life Insurance Benefits in Practice" section in **Chapter 4**).

Pension Plan and Retirement Plan Structures

A range of pension plan and retirement plan structures are available for individuals, depending on their employment status, i.e. employee, self-employed or retired. In general, company owners and employees have similar options for pension planning purposes; however, some important differences exist. (See **Chapter 3** for more information.)

A summary of the main pension plan and retirement plan structures is set out in **Figure 1.5** below.

FIGURE 1.5: PENSION PLAN AND RETIREMENT PLAN STRUCTURES

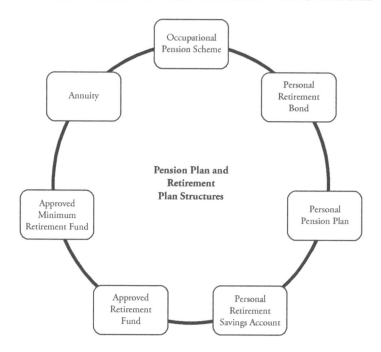

These pension plan and retirement plan structures are discussed in detail in later chapters – a summary of each structure is contained below.

- **Occupational Pension Schemes (OPS)** An occupational pension scheme (OPS) is the most common pension plan structure provided for employees/company owners in employment and is structured as a tax-exempt trust established by an employer for the purposes of providing retirement benefits and/or death benefits for employees. A trust is an arrangement whereby a trustee holds assets for the benefit of beneficiaries (in this case employees). Income and gains earned on the investments in the trust are not subject to tax in Ireland. An OPS can be established as a group arrangement for a number of employees or as a one-person arrangement for a single employee (often used by company owners who wish to have a stand-alone pension plan structure separate to any group structure).

An OPS can be structured to provide retirement benefits on a defined benefit (DB) basis or on a defined contribution (DC) basis. On a DB basis, the benefits are based on years of service and final salary levels. On a DC basis, benefits are based on the value accumulated in investments in the individual's pension plan. (Very few, if any, new DB schemes are being established, and existing DB schemes are increasingly winding up or closing to new entrants due to the open-ended funding commitment to such schemes for employers.)

- **Personal Retirement Bond (PRB)** A PRB, also known as a 'buy-out bond', is used for the transfer payment of an individual's benefit in an OPS, where the individual is leaving the OPS, or the OPS is being wound up. A PRB is typically structured as an insurance policy, or similar, that is purchased by the trustees of an OPS in the name of the individual. A PRB is often used by individuals who have left employment, who have a pension benefit in their former employer's OPS and who wish to have greater flexibility regarding the investment of the assets in the pension plan. In some circumstances, particularly on transferring from a DB scheme, an individual will have more options for taking benefits after transferring to a PRB.

- **Personal Pension Plan (PPP)** A PPP is a pension plan structure most commonly used by self-employed individuals. A PPP is also known as a 'retirement annuity contract' (RAC) and typically consists of an insurance policy taken out by an individual. Life cover can also be provided by a PPP (see **Chapter 6** for more on life insurance).

- **Personal Retirement Savings Account (PRSA)** A PRSA is an individually held retirement savings account that is designed to be used by anyone, regardless of employment status, to save for retirement. Group PRSA plans can be used by employers to provide access to a pension plan for employees. At a minimum, employers must provide employees with access to a PRSA.

- **Approved Retirement Fund (ARF)** An ARF is a post-retirement investment fund that is used to provide an individual with income during retirement, while allowing the individual to maintain beneficial ownership and control of the capital that has been transferred in from their pension plan on retirement.

- **Approved Minimum Retirement Fund (AMRF)** If an individual opts for an ARF on retirement, €63,500 must be invested in an AMRF, unless the individual is receiving other pension income of at least €12,700 per annum. A single income withdrawal of 4% per year is permitted from an AMRF until the AMRF becomes an ARF, which occurs:
  - when the individual is aged 75; or
  - when the individual dies; or
  - if the individual is in receipt of other pension income of at least €12,700 per annum (such as the maximum State pension).

- **Annuity** An annuity is a secure, regular income for life, payable by an insurance company in exchange for all or part of a pension fund as accumulated at retirement. The amount of secure regular income payable will depend on a number of factors, such as the age of the individual, interest rates and bond yields, and the type of secure income required. Annuities are less attractive in a low-interest rate environment, as is the case at the time of writing. Annuity rates are based on long-term bond yields, which in turn are influenced by interest rates. When interest rates are high, long-term bond yields are high, and thus annuity rates are high, and vice versa.

Benefits from a Pension Plan

The benefits from a pension plan include the following:

- **Retirement benefits** The main purpose of a pension plan is to provide benefits in retirement. A number of options are available, consisting of:
  - a lump sum payable on retirement, some or all of which can be tax free;
  - a retirement fund that is invested in order to provide income during retirement (see above);
  - secure regular income during retirement provided by an annuity (see above).

  (See **Chapter 6** for more information on these retirement benefit options.)

- **Death benefits** In the event of death before retirement, benefits from a pension plan are paid out to dependants/next-of-kin. These benefits can consist of a lump sum (subject to limits in specific cases) with the balance (in specific cases) used to provide a dependants' pension. In the event of death in retirement, the benefits payable will depend on the retirement benefits options chosen at the time of retirement. (See **Chapters 3** and **4** for more information.)

- **Ill-health/early-retirement benefits** In the event of an individual becoming ill prior to retirement, retirement benefits can be paid to the individual, subject to specific conditions. (See **Chapter 3** for more information.)

Typical Costs of a Pension Plan

The typical costs of a pension plan can include the costs for administering the plan, the investment manager costs, and the advisor costs. The cost levels depend on a number of factors, such as the size of the plan, advisor fees, the type of investments undertaken by the plan, when the plan was established and the term to normal retirement.

In general, depending on the type of pension plan, the costs can include **some or all** of the following:

1. **Contribution charge** – a percentage charge deducted from each contribution (which can apply to employer and employee contributions).
2. **Annual management charge (AMC)** – a percentage of the value of the assets in the plan, which is typically deducted at source from the pension plan value by the provider of the pension plan.
3. **Plan/policy fees** – administration fees deducted from the plan to cover the costs of ongoing plan administration.
4. **Pensions Authority fees** – payable to the Pensions Authority, the statutory authority in Ireland that monitors the operation of pension plans. These fees vary, depending on the number of employees.
5. **Early exit charges** – these can apply to some plans on transfers out of the plan during an initial period, such as the first five years from the commencement date of the pension plan.
6. **Broker/advisor and other fees** – fees can be payable to the broker/advisor who advises on, arranges and oversees the ongoing operation of the plan. Legal, accountancy and audit fees can also be payable (for pension plans with many members).

Pension plans with many members (such as large employer plans) and/or with significant asset values, tend to have lower charges than plans with fewer members and/or with modest asset values (i.e. economies of scale apply).

Rules and Regulations

In Ireland, a number of statutory bodies oversee the implementation of the rules and regulations governing pension plans, including:

- the Revenue Commissioners (Revenue);
- the Pensions Authority;
- the Financial Services and Pensions Ombudsman (FSPO).

A brief overview of each body's role is set out below.

The Revenue Commissioners

The legislation governing the tax treatment of pensions is contained in the Taxes Consolidation Act 1997 (TCA 1997) (Part 30 and Schedules 23 to 23C). This Act grants discretionary powers to Revenue in relation to the approval of OPS, PPP and PRSA plans.

Revenue publishes a comprehensive technical manual, known as the 'Revenue Pensions Manual', which is available on its website (www.revenue.ie), and which assists pension plan advisors, administrators and other financial advisors.

The Pensions Authority

The Pensions Authority (previously 'the Pensions Board') was established by the Pensions Act 1990 in order to improve governance and oversight of pension plans. The Authority has responsibility to supervise compliance with the requirements of the 1990 Act in relation to OPSs, PRSAs, trust RACs, registered administrators, PRSA providers and employers. The Authority also has the power to investigate suspected beaches of the 1990 Act and to instigate prosecutions where breaches have occurred.

The Pensions Authority has three core functions:

1. **Regulation**: efficient and effective regulation of pension plans and PRSAs.
2. **Policy**: advising the Government on pension policy and development.
3. **Information**: providing guidance and information to the public and for pension trustees and administrators.

The website www.pensionsauthority.ie contains more information on the above functions and activities, and also contains a number of useful guides for consumers, employers and trustees.

Financial Services and Pensions Ombudsman

The role of the Financial Services and Pensions Ombudsman (FSPO) includes investigating and ruling on complaints from pension plan members and beneficiaries. Significantly, the FSPO may award compensation to a complainant. (See www.fspo.ie for more information.)

Developments in the Pensions Landscape

At the time of writing, the Irish pensions landscape looks set to change significantly in the years ahead, as legislators and regulators continue to tackle the challenges arising from an increasingly ageing population.

As mentioned above, the 'promise to pay' pension systems in many European countries, which rely on a younger workforce paying for the pensions of older citizens, are unlikely to be sustainable in their current form over the long term. Instead, a 'hybrid' system may emerge, whereby the State provides a basic level of pension income funded by social insurance contributions (similar to the current state pension systems in Ireland and the UK), to be supplemented by a private pension plan system into which workers are obliged to pay contributions on an ongoing basis.

A number of developments and initiatives have arisen in recent years to tackle the growing financial challenges of providing adequate pensions for citizens in retirement, including:

- the Pensions Roadmap;
- automatic enrolment in a pension plan;
- a pan-European personal pension product (PEPP).

The Pensions Roadmap

In 2018, the Irish Government published *A Roadmap for Pensions Reform 2018–2023*, which proposes comprehensive reform in the following key areas of the Irish pension system:

1. **Reform of the State Pension (Contributory) system** – including a move to a 'total contributions approach' and indexation of the State pension. The total contributions approach differs from the 'yearly averaging' approach, in that the amount of State pension payable to an individual would be directly proportionate to the number of social insurance contributions made by the individual over his or her working life, with significant pension credits granted to people who have taken time out of the workplace to perform caring duties (such as parents caring for children). The pension rate would be indexed to changes in the consumer price index (CPI) and in average wages.

2. **An 'automatic enrolment system'** – to be introduced by 2022, with contributions from the employer and the employee, with the State also providing a matching contribution. (See below for further information on what is generally known as 'auto enrolment'.)

3. **Improved governance and regulation** – including the implementa-tion of the EU Directive on the activities and supervision of insti-tutions for occupational retirement provision (known as the 'IORP II Directive'), more powers for the Pensions Authority, new stan-dards for trustees, a review of ARFs, and the introduction of 'Master Trusts' (single trust arrangements that can provide pensions plans for many employers, rather than each employer arranging an indi-vidual trust, as is typically the case at the time of writing).
4. **Support for defined benefit (DB) schemes** – including a standard approach in winding up DB schemes and improved levels of pro-tection for scheme members and beneficiaries, to help ensure that the benefits arising from the wind up of a DB scheme are fairly distributed.
5. **Public sector pensions** – including the Pension Related Deduction (PRD) to be converted to a permanent Additional Superannuation Contribution and increasing the compulsory retirement age for pub-lic servants to 70 for those recruited before 1 April 2004. The PRD was introduced in 2009 as a temporary additional deduction from the pay of public sector workers to assist the State with the cost of public-sector pensions. The proposed Additional Superannuation Contribution would be permanent and would replace the tempo-rary PRD.
6. **Retirement readiness** – including the development of a proposal for a deferral scheme within the State Pension (Contributory), with an increased amount of State pension being paid to those who defer taking the State pension, in order to encourage and support individ-uals who wish to continue working beyond the normal retirement age.

Automatic Enrolment

The Pensions Roadmap includes a proposal to introduce an 'automatic enrolment', or auto-enrolment, pension plan system in Ireland by 2022, with the following guideline parameters, subject to consultation and agreement:

- All employees in the private sector over identified age and income thresholds (e.g. 23 years of age and €20,000 per year), and without existing private pension provision, will be automatically enrolled into the system.
- Workers on lower salaries, self-employed workers and workers with existing private pension provision will be able to opt into the system.

- Contributions into the system will be made by both employees and employers, and the State will top up these contributions.
- Employees automatically enrolled in the system will be allowed to opt-out following a minimum period of participation (e.g. nine months) and any contributions made by the employee during the minimum period will be refunded.
- The exact ratio of contributions by the employee, the employer and the State is to be determined during the design phase. As an example, starting from a modest base and automatically escalating on a scheduled basis over a period of time, employers could be asked to match employee contributions euro-for-euro, subject to an eventual upper limit on employer contributions of 6% of gross salary. Similarly, the State may match employee contributions on a 1:3 basis. In such a scenario, an employee making a personal contribution of 6% of salary would see that contribution matched by an employer contribution of 6% and a State contribution of 2%, bringing the total contribution into the fund to 14% of salary. Any contributions made by the State may replace, rather than augment, existing tax reliefs.
- Retirement benefits accrued under the system will become payable at the age the individual reaches when their State Pension (Contributory) becomes payable.
- Workers with pre-existing personal or occupational pension arrangements will be able to retain those arrangements.

In the UK, automatic enrolment of employees in pension schemes commenced in 2012. All employees over the age of 22 and below the State pension age must be enrolled into a pension scheme, provided that they earn over a specific amount per week or month.

The automatic enrolment minimum contribution in the UK is 8% of earnings, consisting of 4% payable by the employee, 3% payable by the employer, and 1% payable by the State (via tax relief). For the 2020–2021 tax year, the 'qualifying earnings' band is between £6,240 and £50,000. This means the first £6,240 of an employee's earnings do not count for the purposes of automatic enrolment.

In addition, earnings need to be at or above £10,000 per annum before automatic enrolment is triggered. Qualifying earnings are based on gross earnings and include bonuses, commission, overtime and any statutory pay, such as sick pay or maternity pay.

In Australia, the nationwide superannuation, or 'super' system, commenced in the early 1990s, with mandatory employer contributions at 9.50% of employee earnings. The 'Super' is generally viewed as one of the world's most successful retirement income systems.

The Pan-European Personal Pension Product (PEPP)

The European Union has provided a framework for the creation of a pan-European personal pension product, or 'PEPP' (via Regulation (EU) 2019/1238). This framework is a welcome development, as EU Members States currently have a range of individual pension plan systems that are often not compatible with each other, making cross-border pension plan transfers difficult to arrange in practice.

The PEPP creates a pension plan standard that will apply to pension plans throughout the EU, to facilitate individuals with combining their pension plan benefits that may have been accrued from working in different EU Member States.

10 KEY POINTS: PENSION PLANNING

1. Long-term financial planning objectives should include having an adequate level of pension income, being debt free and having accessible savings and/or investments.
2. State pension systems are unlikely to be sustainable in their current form in the decades to come.
3. A pension plan is a tax-efficient savings and investment structure approved by the Revenue Commissioners to provide financial benefits during retirement or on death.
4. Financial benefits from a pension plan are in addition to State pension entitlements.
5. For every €3 of your cash that you pay into your pension plan, the State can pay in up to €2, in the form of personal income tax relief.
6. The 'half your age rule' entails that the percentage of your earnings paid into a pension plan should be half your age throughout your working life. An alternative approach is to 'save more tomorrow' by increasing pension contributions by 1–2% of earnings each year.
7. A range of pension plan and retirement plan structures are available for individuals, depending on their employment status, i.e. employee, self-employed or retired.
8. Employers can make contributions to employee pension plans, which are allowable as a trading expense for business tax purposes and are not subject to employer PRSI.

9. Benefits from pension plans can include a tax-free lump sum on retirement, a secure regular income in retirement and benefits in the event of death or ill health.
10. The pensions landscape is changing, with developments such as the Pensions Roadmap containing proposals for comprehensive reform for pensions in Ireland, including a proposal to introduce an auto-enrolment system. The European Union has provided a framework for the creation of a PEPP (a pan-European personal pension product).

2.

Investment Assets and Strategies

- Introduction
- Investment Assets
- Investment Risk and Investment Volatility
- The Importance of Diversification
- An Appropriate Investment Strategy
- Investment Strategies in Pension Plans

Introduction

A pension plan is an investment savings plan that has the objective of generating a return on money paid in by typically investing across a wide range of assets. Many pension plans consist of a portfolio of individual investment assets (such as shares, bonds, property and cash) managed by investment managers. The value of these investments can rise and fall over time, depending on economic and investment cycles and other factors.

The focus in this chapter is on **defined contribution pension plans**, which is a type of pension plan into which contributions are paid in order to build up a fund to be used to pay out benefits in retirement (or on death).

The following topics are covered in this chapter:

- investment assets;
- investment risk and investment volatility;
- the importance of diversification;
- an appropriate investment strategy;
- investment strategies in pension plans.

Investment Assets

Pension plans invest in a wide range of investment assets. Every month, multiple millions are paid into pension plans all over the world. The investment managers of these pension plans have the responsibility of investing this cash in assets that provide the potential to generate returns on investment over time.

Accordingly, pension plans are among the world's largest owners of physical assets. For example, pension plans own:

- many office blocks, shopping centres, business parks and industrial estates;
- large proportions of government debt issued in the form of government bonds;
- large holdings in many companies that are listed on stock exchanges around the world.

Pension plans generally 'spread' the investments across a range of investment assets across the globe in order to reduce the risk of over-exposure to any individual investment and/or individual region.

Many pension plans hold hundreds or even thousands of individual investments.

The most common investment structures held by pension plans are pooled investment funds, whereby monies from many individual investors are combined or 'pooled' together for the purposes of investment.

A summary of the main investment asset types and their indicative risk/volatility and return potential is shown in **Figure 2.1** below.

FIGURE 2.1: INVESTMENT RETURNS AND RISK/VOLATILITY

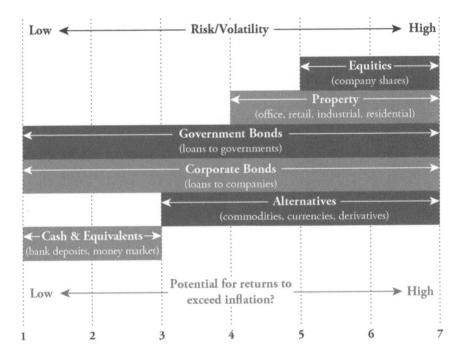

- **Equities**: 'equities' is the generic name for the shares of companies listed on stock markets. Equities can provide returns for investors in two ways, i.e. by an increase in the underlying value of the company, represented by an increase in its share price, and by the payment of surplus profits to investors in the form of dividends.

  Equities are classed as **high-risk** investments, the value of which can fall significantly as well as rise. Despite their volatile nature, equities are generally viewed as the most appropriate assets for delivering returns in aggregate that can exceed inflation over the long term. (See below for further discussion of investment risk and investment volatility.)

- **Property**: pension plans invest in individual properties, such as office blocks, which are typically rented to tenants and generate a rental income for the pension plan. In addition, pension plans can invest in portfolios of property indirectly, by investing in specialist property funds or companies that, in turn, own individual properties.

  Property values are influenced by a wide range of factors, and past experience in Ireland and other countries has highlighted the risks of investing in property that becomes overvalued. The risk profile of property investments depends on many factors, such as the location of the property, the quality of the tenant, the terms of the lease, the availability of bank debt, interest rates, the economic environment, etc. In general, the risk profile of property investments can be viewed as **medium risk,** with some property investments classed as **high** to **very high risk**.

- **Bonds (including government bonds and corporate bonds)**: a bond is a debt instrument whereby investors make a loan to the issuer by purchasing a security known as a 'bond'. The issuer (e.g. a country or a company) typically undertakes to pay the investor a regular rate of interest (coupon) and typically undertakes to pay back the nominal value of the loan at a specified date in the future (redemption date). Bonds issued by countries are known as 'government bonds' and bonds issued by companies are known as 'corporate bonds'.

  Bonds are bought and sold by investors on an ongoing basis. The market value of a bond can increase or decrease during the period prior to its redemption date. A wide range of factors influence the price of a bond, such as the financial health of the issuer, the general economic climate, the duration of the bond, interest rates, etc. Depending on the quality of the issuer and the specific terms of the bond, the risk profile of bonds can range from **very low risk** (e.g. short-dated government bonds issued by financially strong countries) to **very high risk** (e.g. bonds issued by countries or companies that are in financial difficulty).

- **Cash and cash equivalents**: the cash holdings of pension plans are typically invested in 'money market' funds. Rather than investing in a single cash instrument such as a deposit with a single bank, in order to spread the risk, a money market fund invests in a wide range of cash instruments, such as a range of short-dated, blue-chip government and corporate bonds from a number of issuers, and/or a range of short-term deposits with different banks.

  The returns from cash investments in money market funds are typically similar to or lower than the European Central Bank (ECB) base interest rate. Some pension plans can provide access to deposits from

31

individual banks, which may provide a return that is higher than the return from money market funds. The risk profile of pension plan holdings in money market funds is typically **very low risk** – the risk profile of a deposit from an individual bank is higher than a money market fund and can be viewed as **low risk**, depending on the financial security of the bank.

'CAPITAL SECURE' INVESTMENTS

Some investments, such as cash deposits, State Savings and government bonds at maturity, have 'capital security' as a key feature. However, investors should note that capital security, i.e. where the provider of the investment 'promises' to pay some or all of the original capital, depends on the ability of the provider to honour their promise. In nearly all cases, the investment made by the investor will be in the form of a loan to the provider, e.g. a bank deposit is a loan to a bank, State Savings are loans to the State, etc.

If the provider is unable to meet its obligations, investors can lose some or all of their original capital, as has happened in the case of bank failures (e.g. the Lehman Brothers collapse in 2008) and when governments default on the repayment of bonds (e.g. the collapse of the Russian stock, bond and currency markets in 1998).

In reality, a cast-iron, risk-free capital secure investment does not exist, and investors should evaluate the 'security' of all capital secure investments.

The four assets classes described above – equities, property, bonds and cash – are the assets in which traditional pension plans invest. These traditional pension plans typically adopt a 'buy and hold' strategy, i.e. buying assets with the expectation that the assets will generate an income and/or rise in value over time. This strategy does not include investing in 'alternative' assets or strategies that can protect the value of assets in falling markets, or that can even generate returns in falling markets.

Alternative Assets

Pension plans can invest in **alternative assets** and strategies in order to provide greater diversification (see below). 'Alternatives' is a generic term for assets or strategies that do not necessarily fit into the categories of traditional investments in equities, bonds, properties or cash. A brief summary of the some of the alternative assets typically used is given below.

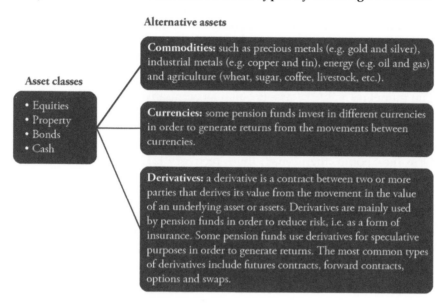

Alternative assets

Asset classes

- Equities
- Property
- Bonds
- Cash

Commodities: such as precious metals (e.g. gold and silver), industrial metals (e.g. copper and tin), energy (e.g. oil and gas) and agriculture (wheat, sugar, coffee, livestock, etc.).

Currencies: some pension funds invest in different currencies in order to generate returns from the movements between currencies.

Derivatives: a derivative is a contract between two or more parties that derives its value from the movement in the value of an underlying asset or assets. Derivatives are mainly used by pension funds in order to reduce risk, i.e. as a form of insurance. Some pension funds use derivatives for speculative purposes in order to generate returns. The most common types of derivatives include futures contracts, forward contracts, options and swaps.

Investment Risk and Investment Volatility

Investment risk can be defined in different ways. In simple terms, it can be viewed as the likelihood or probability of an investment losing value.

Investment volatility can also be defined in different ways. In simple terms, it is the rate or pace at which the value or price of an asset moves up and down.

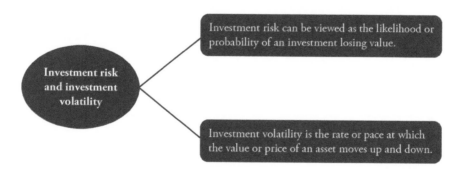

Investment risk and investment volatility

Investment risk can be viewed as the likelihood or probability of an investment losing value.

Investment volatility is the rate or pace at which the value or price of an asset moves up and down.

33

Investment risk and investment volatility are not necessarily the same thing, and investors can sometimes confuse these terms. For example, an investment fund that invests in the shares of hundreds of large companies listed on stock markets will likely have a high level of volatility, in that the value of the fund will likely move up and down on a frequent basis. However, the chances of this fund permanently losing value over the long term and never recovering is low, therefore the 'investment risk' of this investment is not necessarily the same as its volatility.

The monetary value of assets (such as company shares, property, etc.) tends to increase in value over the 'long term' (typically a period of seven years or longer). Residential property price movements in Ireland in recent years highlight the volatility of assets in the short/medium term (i.e. 'boom' then 'bust', then 'recovery'). However, in aggregate, residential property values in Ireland are far higher today compared to 20, 30, or 40 years ago.

Human behaviour (which can be irrational) can distort the market value of an asset in the short to medium term, but over the long term the market value of an asset should reflect its intrinsic fundamental value.

Investment risk and volatility become more important for our savings and/or investments as we move closer to the time when we are likely to start spending those investments. Conversely, investment risk and volatility are less important when we are further away from that time.

Individual pension investors will have different **risk/volatility profiles**, depending on personal preferences, the age of the individual, personal objectives and other factors. (See **Figure 2.3** below for more information.)

To assist investors with assessing the risk or volatility of an investment fund, a stated risk or volatility level for an individual fund will typically be provided by the fund manager/provider. A standardised approach for measuring volatility has been developed by the European Securities and Markets Authority (ESMA), which is an independent authority established to safeguard the stability of the EU's financial system. This standardised approach consists of a seven-point scale of very low to very high risk, with '1' being very low risk and '7' being very high risk – and many investment funds will have a risk rating based on this ESMA scale (see **Figure 2.2** below).

FIGURE 2.2: THE ESMA RISK-RATING SCALE

| 1 | 2 | 3 | 4 | 5 | 6 | 7 |
| Lower risk | | | Medium risk | | | Higher risk |

Under the ESMA methodology, risk is measured by using the weekly past returns of an investment fund over a five-year period. The methodology involves 'looking back' over the previous five years to determine the level of volatility over this period.

Although this methodology can be a useful indicator, the past performance of an investment asset is often **not** a reliable guide to future performance.

MARKET BEHAVIOUR

Financial markets, such as a stock market or a bond market, operate in a similar way to most markets, in that the market is a place where potential buyers and sellers come together to transact.

The price of an item for sale in a market is typically determined by supply of and demand for the item. Irrational human behaviour (which can often occur in 'boom' and 'bust' times) can drive up or down the price of an item, whereby the price becomes distorted and does not reflect the intrinsic value of the item.

The challenge for long-term investors is to pay less attention to short-term price fluctuations, and instead focus on the potential long-term intrinsic value of investment assets. A pension/financial advisor should help their client to focus on the long-term returns on investments in their pension plan, with less focus on short-term events.

The Importance of Diversification

As a strategy, diversification is often described as 'not having all your eggs in one basket'. The values of different types of investment assets do not always move in the same direction. Diversification within an investment portfolio is an approach whereby different kinds of investments are held, on the basis that over the long term the portfolio of investments in aggregate will generate a similar or higher return with lower risk, compared to a single investment within the portfolio.

For example, during the financial crisis of 2007 to 2009, the values of company shares fell significantly, whereas the value of bonds issued by financially secure countries (such as Germany) rose. Accordingly, the effect of falls in the value of company shares within an investment portfolio would have been mitigated by the rise in the value of such bonds if both were held in the same portfolio.

Most investors, including investment managers, cannot buy and sell investment assets at the most opportune times on a consistent basis over the long term, as events that influence investment markets cannot be predicted with certainty. Therefore, in accepting the fact that the future is uncertain and unpredictable, diversification can protect the value of an investment portfolio in volatile times.

Diversification can be implemented in a number of ways. In the simplest terms, a portfolio that has two investments is more diversified than a portfolio that has a single investment. However, if the two investments are similar, for example shares in two companies in the same region in the same sector (e.g. Bank of Ireland and AIB), the benefit of such diversification will be limited, as the value of both investments may move in the same direction over the long term, i.e. both investments have a high degree of **correlation** with each other.

In this example of investing in shares in Bank of Ireland and AIB, the next step would be to add investments in **different sectors** in **different regions**, for example, in global technology companies, such as Apple or Microsoft, that are not correlated with the Irish banking sector.

However, even though this portfolio of shares may be diversified across sectors and regions, the portfolio is still invested in a single asset class, i.e. equities (company shares) – and equities in aggregate can move in a similar direction, particularly in a downturn or crisis. The portfolio can be further diversified by adding investments from **different asset classes**, such as government bonds, corporate bonds, commodities or property, which are not necessarily correlated with equities. The portfolio can be further protected by using 'alternatives', such as **options,** as insurance against negative market movements.

EXAMPLE 2.1: A DIVERSIFIED INVESTMENT PORTFOLIO

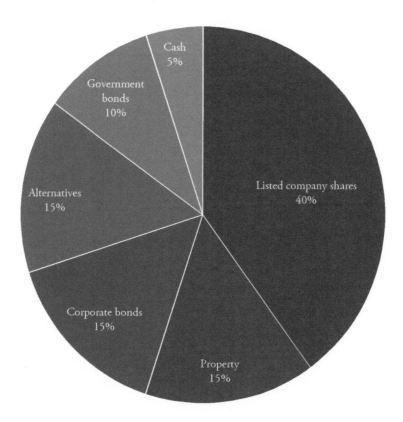

An Appropriate Investment Strategy

As with all investment portfolios, the appropriate strategy for the individual investor will depend on many factors, some of which are illustrated in **Figure 2.3**.

FIGURE 2.3: AN APPROPRIATE INVESTMENT STRATEGY DEPENDS ON ...

Objectives of the investor	Term of the investment	Investment risk / volatility profile	Other savings and investments
Preserving capital or exceeding inflation – which is more important?	*How long until you need to access the investment?*	*Tolerance for potential losses in order to make potential gains*	*The value and type of other savings and investments*
For most pension investors, the main reason for investing is to accumulate an investment value that can deliver a return that at least matches, but preferably exceeds, inflation over the long term. For most pension investors approaching retirement or already in retirement, objectives can differ to those of younger pension investors; preserving the value in the pension plan and generating a regular retirement income can be more important.	Investors with long-term horizons (typically at least 7–10 years) may be more comfortable with taking more risk, compared to investors with short/medium-term horizons (typically less than 5 years) for whom capital preservation rather than investment growth may be more important. In general, the longer the investment term, the higher the level of investment risk/volatility that may be appropriate, and vice versa.	In general, higher risk investments are more volatile and provide greater potential for investment gains and losses, compared to lower-risk investments, which typically provide lower and more stable returns with less risk to original capital. The returns from lower-risk investments generally do not match or exceed inflation over the long term, so 'playing it safe' can result in the purchasing power of investments falling over time.	The value and type of savings and investments (if any) that an investor already has in place should be considered when determining an investment strategy for a pension plan. For example, if an investor already has exposure to high-risk investments, such as shares, a more diversified approach may be appropriate in order to reduce the investor's reliance on the performance of a specific type or 'class' of investment.

Investment Strategies in Pension Plans

Pension plans can adopt a number of strategies in order to allocate funds across different investment assets, i.e. in order to determine the 'asset allocation' of the pension plan.

The assets within a pension plan are typically managed on a 'passive' basis or an 'active' basis (see **Figure 2.4**).

FIGURE 2.4: PASSIVE VS ACTIVE INVESTMENT MANAGEMENT

Passive investment management	Active investment management
• Objective: to 'duplicate' market returns by investing in assets in proportions that closely match or track the chosen market.	• Objective: to 'beat' market returns by investing in assets the investment manager believes will beat the chosen market.
• Example: a US equity index fund may track the S&P 500 Index.	• Example: a US equity active fund may aim to beat the S&P 500 Index.
• Investment manager charges can be lower than actively managed funds, as research or additional expertise may not be required.	• The investment manager charges can be higher than passively managed funds due to the cost of research and additional expertise that may be employed.

Asset allocation is the most important determinant of long-term investment returns. Pension plan investment managers use a number of asset allocation strategies, including:

* a lifestyle investment strategy;
* a multi-asset risk target strategy;
* a managed fund strategy;
* a target-return strategy;
* specific-asset strategies.

Lifestyle Investment Strategy

A **lifestyle investment strategy** automatically alters the underlying mix of the investment assets in the pension plan based on the investor's term to retirement. The longer the term to retirement, the higher the proportion invested in growth assets such as equities, which are high-risk/return assets. The allocation to growth assets is automatically reduced and the allocation to lower risk/return assets, such as bonds and cash, is automatically increased as the investor moves towards retirement.

Accordingly, as an investor approaches retirement, most of their funds should be invested in low-risk assets. The rationale behind this strategy is that investors may benefit from taking more risk in their pension plan in the earlier years, but may benefit from and prefer stability over volatility as retirement age approaches.

This approach is typically the 'default' strategy for many pension plans, particularly group employee pension plans.

The chart in **Example 2.2** below shows a lifestyle investment strategy in practice, available through New Ireland Assurance and managed by State Street Global Advisors, which automatically de-risks over the 15-year period prior to an investor's normal retirement age (typically age 60 or 65).

EXAMPLE 2.2: A LIFESTYLE INVESTMENT STRATEGY

Higher growth, higher risk/volatility

Term to Retirement	Equities	Property	Corporate bonds	Government bonds	PRIME 3	Cash
15+ years to Retirement	70%	5%	17%	8%		
15 years to Retirement	70%	5%	17%	8%		
14 years	68%	5%	18%	9%		
13 years	66%	5%	19%	10%		
12 years	64%	5%	21%	10%		
11 years	62%	5%	22%	11%		
10 years to Retirement	60%	5%	23%	12%		
9 years	54%	5%	24%	12%	5%	
8 years	48%	5%	25%	12%	10%	
7 years	42%	5%	25%	13%	15%	
6 years	36%	5%	26%	13%	20%	
5 years to Retirement	30%	5%	27%	13%	25%	
4 years	24%	4%	21%	11%	35%	5%
3 years	18%	3%	16%	7%	45%	10%
2 years	12%	2%	11%	5%	55%	15%
1 years	6%	1%	5%	3%	65%	20%
At Retirement					75%	25%

Lower growth, lower risk/volatility

■ Equities ■ Property ■ Corporate bonds
■ Government bonds ■ PRIME 3 ■ Cash

Pension investors are grouped together based on their expected year of retirement.

The investment strategy recognises that individual investment needs may differ depending on the term to retirement. The strategy is designed to match changing needs by moving from assets with a higher level of risk when the pension investor is further from retirement to assets with a lower level of risk as they near retirement.

An important feature is that pension investors do not have to make any decisions about what funds to invest in, or when fund switches or assets switches should be made.

'PRIME 3' in the chart above is a diversified portfolio with a 3 out of 7 risk/volatility rating, i.e. a low-medium risk/volatility profile.

Source: www.newireland.ie/pensions/pension-funds-performance/(with the permission of New Ireland)

Lifestyle investment strategy

A lifestyle investment strategy is typically the default strategy for many pension plans, particularly group employee pension plans.

Multi-asset Risk Target Strategy

A **multi-asset risk target strategy** typically consists of a range of funds with specific risk target objectives, ranging from low risk to high risk. An investor selects a fund that has a risk profile in line with the investor's own risk profile. The fund manager has a specific risk target within which to manage the fund, and each fund is rebalanced on a regular basis to ensure that its risk profile remains unchanged. Risk target funds are multi-asset funds, i.e. the fund invests in a wide range of investment assets. **Example 2.3** below illustrates a multi-asset risk target strategy in practice, in this case the range of five multi-asset portfolios (MAPs) with different risk targets available through Irish Life.

The rationale behind this strategy is that investment assets have different risk profiles at different times. For example, commercial property was viewed as a stable, income-generating, low-to-medium risk investment until the property market crash in the aftermath of the financial crisis of 2008. Commercial property is now generally viewed as being a medium/high-risk investment. As the risk profile of managed funds (as discussed in the next section) can change at different times, such funds can become unsuitable for investors who first invested based on the fund's original risk profile. A multi-asset risk target strategy endeavours to address this issue by altering the asset mix of the fund on an ongoing basis to ensure that the fund stays within the stated risk profile.

EXAMPLE 2.3: IRISH LIFE MULTI-ASSET PORTFOLIOS

Risk rating	2 Careful	3 Conservative	4 Balanced	5 Experienced	6 Adventurous	7 Very adventurous
Fund name	Multi-asset portfolio 2	Multi-asset portfolio 3	Multi-asset portfolio 4	Multi-asset portfolio 5	Multi-asset portfolio 6	

■ Cash ■ Bonds ■ Shares ■ Others and External managers

Source: https://www.irishlife.ie/investments/irish-life-maps (with the permission of Irish Life)

In addition, multi-asset risk target funds can employ additional risk-management techniques that can reduce exposure to equities when volatility is high, and vice versa.

Managed Fund Strategy

The **managed fund strategy** is a long-established, traditional invest-ment strategy that consists of allocating (pension) funds across the four main asset classes, i.e. equities, bonds, property and cash. This strat-egy is based on the view that, as equities deliver the best returns over the long term, a managed fund should typically hold between 50% and 90% in equities, with diversification being achieved by also holding some bonds, property and cash. The performance of each fund man-ager is usually ranked against the performance of a peer group of simi-lar fund managers. Managed fund strategies can employ a 'consensus' approach, whereby the asset allocation within the fund aims to match the average asset allocation of the main managed funds in the market.

The strategy worked well during the 1980s and 1990s, which was a period of strong and stable investment returns. However, the more volatile environment of the 2000s exposed the limitations of the strategy in terms of adapting to rapidly changing investment conditions in order to protect investor capital. Managed funds typically have a medium- to high-risk profile, due to their significant exposure to equities.

Target-return Strategy

In a target-return strategy, the investment manager has a target of achieving a specific return over the medium-to-long term. The target return is typically expressed as a specific return that is higher than cash returns, for example, a target annualised return of cash returns + 4% over a rolling five-year period.

In order to achieve the target return, investment managers can have a broad mandate to invest in a wide range of investment assets and strategies, including alternative assets such as derivatives, which can be used as a form of insurance against falling asset values and can also be used to enhance returns from underlying investment assets.

Specific-asset Strategies

A **specific-asset strategy** is an investment strategy that focuses on a type of asset or sector, such as:

- company shares listed on a single stock market, e.g. the Irish stock market;
- company shares listed on regional stock markets, e.g. European stock markets;
- commercial property;
- government bonds;
- corporate bonds, i.e. loans issued by companies and other commercial entities;
- commodities.

An example of a specific-asset strategy is the Irish Commercial Property Fund managed by Aviva, which invests in commercial property in Ireland, consisting mainly of offices and retail properties in Dublin. The objective of the fund is to deliver long-term returns through a combination of rental income and capital growth, with property development opportunities.

Commercial property funds are mainly actively managed rather than passively managed. Aviva summarises the active management approach for the Irish Commercial Property Fund in **Example 2.4** below.

EXAMPLE 2.4: AN ACTIVELY MANAGED, SPECIFIC-ASSET INVESTMENT FUND

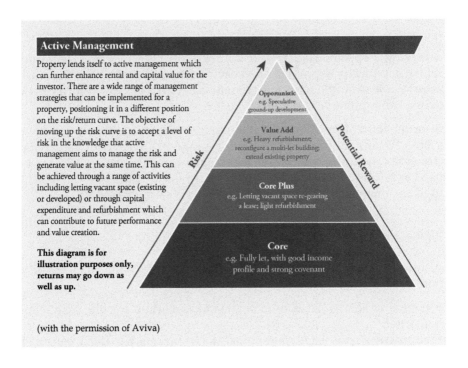

(with the permission of Aviva)

10 KEY POINTS: INVESTMENT ASSETS AND STRATEGIES

1. A pension plan is an investment savings plan that invests across a wide range of investment assets, such as shares, bonds, property and cash.

2. Pension plans generally 'spread' the investments across a range of investment assets across the globe in order to reduce the risk of over-exposure to any individual investment and/or individual region. Many pension plans hold hundreds or even thousands of individual investments.

3. The most common investment structures held by pension plans are pooled investment funds, whereby monies from many individual investors are combined or 'pooled' together for the purposes of investment.

4. In addition to shares, bonds, property and cash, pension plans can also invest in alternative assets and strategies in order to provide greater diversification. 'Alternatives' is a generic term for assets or strategies that do not necessarily fit into the categories of traditional investments in equities, bonds, properties or cash.

5. 'Investment risk' can be viewed as the likelihood or probability of an investment losing value. 'Investment volatility' is the rate or pace at which the value or price of an asset moves up and down. Both can become more important closer to the time an individual is likely to start spending savings/investments.

6. Individual pension investors will have different risk profiles, depending on personal preferences, the age of the individual, personal objectives and other factors.

7. The challenge for long-term investors (such as most pension plan investors) is to pay less attention to short-term price fluctuations, and instead focus on the potential long-term intrinsic value of investment assets.

8. Diversification in a portfolio of investments in aggregate can generate a similar return with lower risk, compared to a single investment within the portfolio.

9. Pension plans can adopt a number of strategies in order to allocate funds across different investment assets, i.e. in order to determine the 'asset allocation' of the pension plan. These assets are typically managed on a 'passive' basis or an 'active' basis

10. A lifestyle investment strategy automatically alters the underlying mix of the investment assets in a pension fund based on the investor's term to retirement. This strategy is typically the default strategy for many pension plans, particularly group employee pension plans.

3.

Pension Planning for Sole Traders, Partners and Company Owners

- Introduction
- Pension Plans for Self-employed Business Owners
- Additional Pension Plan Options for Company Owners
- Occupational Pension Schemes
- Pension Plan Transfers
- Self-administered/Self-directed Pension Plan Structures

Introduction

Pension planning is a very important method of extracting some of the income generated by a business in order to provide retirement benefits for the business owner. The pension planning options available to self-employed business owners (i.e. sole traders, partners and company owners) typically depend on the legal structure of the business. In general, a corporate structure, such as a private limited company, can provide the most flexible structure for tax-efficient pension planning. Self-employed business owners that operate on a sole trader or partnership basis can also avail of flexible pension planning options.

The following topics are covered in this chapter:

- pension plans for self-employed business owners;
- additional pension plan options for company owners;
- occupational pension schemes (OPSs);
- pension plan transfers;
- self-administered/self-directed pension plan structures.

Pension Plans for Self-employed Business Owners

The pension plan options available for self-employed business owners depend on the structure of the business. Self-employed business owners can operate their business in the following ways:

1. On a sole trader/partnership basis, i.e. income earned from a trade or a profession that is taxable under Schedule D of the Income Tax Acts.
2. As a company owner/shareholder. The company owner must be in receipt of income from the company that is taxable under Schedule E of the Income Tax Acts, i.e. taxable as PAYE income such as salary, directors fees, etc., to avail of the OPS pension plan option (as discussed further on in this chapter).

Two types of pension plan structures are available for all business owners, i.e. a personal pension plan (PPP) and a personal retirement savings account (PRSA). Both structures are similar in terms of contribution levels and retirement benefits (though a PPP can provide a wider range of investment options in some cases). A company owner in receipt of income taxable under Schedule E (such as salary) also has the option of using an occupational pension scheme (OPS) structure, which is the most common pension plan structure used by such company owners.

FIGURE 3.1: PENSION PLANS FOR SELF-EMPLOYED BUSINESS OWNERS

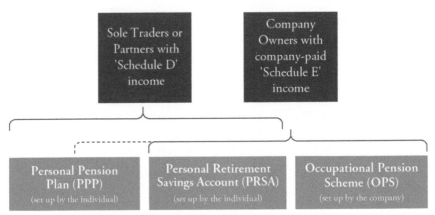

* A company owner can set up a PPP if in "non-pensionable" employment, but not a commonly used option in practice.

> *Note:* While this chapter focuses on 'one-person/one-member' pension plan options for self-employed business owners, the information on the PRSA structure and the OPS structure contained in this chapter is also relevant and applicable for all individuals in employment (with some exceptions, as noted). **Chapter 4** focuses on options for groups of employees (i.e. more than one person), consisting of a group PRSA and a group OPS.

Personal Pension Plans (PPPs)

A personal pension plan (PPP) is a pension plan structure commonly used by sole traders or partners in a partnership. Also known as a 'retirement annuity contract' (RAC), a PPP consists of an insurance policy structure taken out by a self-employed individual.

Individuals in non-pensionable employment (i.e. where the employer does not provide an OPS for employees) can also arrange a PPP.

PPP structures are available through life insurance companies, which typically provide access to a wide range of investment options, including low-, medium- and high-risk investment funds and 'self-directed' investment options (see "Self-administered/Self-directed Pension Plan Structures" section at the end of this chapter).

Life cover can also be arranged with a PPP, either as part of the PPP (associated cover), or set up as a stand-alone policy, under the terms of section 785 of the Taxes Consolidation Act 1997 (TCA 1997). Tax relief is available on premiums paid to a standalone life cover policy set up under section 785 in the same manner as contributions to a PPP. In addition, income protection/disability cover can be arranged as a stand-alone policy to provide an ongoing income in the event of illness or injury, and tax relief on the premiums is also available. (See **Chapter 5** for more information on life insurance options.)

Personal Retirement Savings Accounts (PRSAs)

A personal retirement savings account (PRSA) is an individually held retirement savings account that is designed to be used by all persons, including self-employed individuals (i.e. sole traders/partners) and individuals in employment (including company owners), to save for retirement.

PRSAs were introduced in 2002 in order to encourage more people to save for their retirement by providing a simplified pension structure with a low minimum contribution level and with capped charges (see below). PRSAs are accessible for most people, as contributions can be as low as €10 (per electronic payment).

PRSAs are typically used by self-employed individuals and by individuals who are in non-pensionable employment (i.e. the employer does not provide an OPS for employees). As PRSAs are flexible pension plan structures, the value of a PRSA can be transferred into an OPS provided by an employer. For example, a sole trader/partner becoming an employee can transfer the value of their PRSA into the OPS of their new employer, without incurring any penalties. Employees in an OPS also have the option of using a PRSA for the payment of additional pension contributions (known as AVCs).

Two types of PRSA structures are available as follows:

1. **Standard PRSA**, which can only invest in pooled investment funds and for which the charges are capped at a maximum contribution charge of 5% and a maximum annual charge of 1% of the value of the assets in the PRSA (a 'contribution charge' is a percentage of the contributions, which is deducted by the provider).
2. **Non-Standard PRSA**, which can provide a wider range of investment options, and for which the charges above are not capped.

Transfer charges **cannot** be applied to transfers in or out of a PRSA and additional charges **cannot** be applied in the case of suspending, resuming or varying contributions to a PRSA.

Tax-allowable Contributions

When an individual makes personal contributions to a PPP or a PRSA, personal tax relief can be claimed on these contributions. However, maximum 'tax-allowable' limits – linked to age and a percentage of net earnings – apply to personal contributions that can be made to a PPP and to a PRSA. A table of age-related percentages of 'net relevant earnings', i.e. earnings on which tax is payable, is provided in **Figure 3.2**. The maximum limits apply to annual earnings up to €115,000 – tax relief is not available on personal pension contributions paid in respect of annual earnings above this earnings cap of €115,000. As discussed later in this chapter, employer/company paid contributions to an OPS are not subject to these limits.

FIGURE 3.2: AGE-RELATED PERCENTAGE LIMITS FOR TAX RELIEF

Age	Contribution Limits for Tax Relief (% of net relevant earnings)
Under 30	15%
30 to 39	20%
40 to 49	25%
50 to 54	30%
55 to 59	35%
60+	40%

Tax relief is granted at an individual's higher (i.e. highest) income tax/ PAYE rate, subject to having sufficient net relevant earnings taxed at the higher rate. See **Example 3.1** below.

EXAMPLE 3.1: MAXIMUM TAX-ALLOWABLE PERSONAL PENSION CONTRIBUTIONS

Jack is a sole trader, is taxed as a single person and has net relevant earnings of €30,000. He makes a personal pension contribution of €3,000.

Jack's earnings of €30,000 are subject to income tax at the standard rate (20%). Therefore, Jack can claim tax relief of €600 on his pension contribution (i.e. pension contribution of €3,000 × income tax rate of 20% = €600). In other words, income tax at 20% is calculated on €27,000, not €30,000.

If Jack had net relevant earnings of at least €3,000 above the standard rate band (the standard rate band is €35,300 in 2020), for example net relevant earnings of at least €38,300 in 2020, Jack could claim tax relief of €1,200 on his personal pension contribution (i.e. pension contribution of €3,000 × higher income tax rate of 40% = €1,200).

The impact of the earnings cap is shown in **Example 3.2** below.

EXAMPLE 3.2: TAX RELIEF AND THE EARNINGS CAP

Two 40-year-old self-employed individuals with different levels of earnings as follows:

- The first individual has net relevant annual earnings of €60,000, therefore the maximum tax-allowable pension contribution is €15,000 (i.e. 25% × €60,000).
- The second individual has net relevant annual earnings of €200,000, therefore the maximum tax-allowable pension contribution is €28,750 (i.e. 25% × the earnings cap of €115,000).

The first individual can make the maximum tax-allowable contribution without further restriction – the maximum tax-allowable contribution for the second individual is further restricted due to the €115,000 earnings cap.

Relevant Earnings and Net Relevant Earnings

'Relevant earnings' and 'net relevant earnings' are specifically defined in legislation. 'Relevant earnings' include the following:

- income from a trade;
- income from a profession;

- foreign income from a trade, profession or employment;
- earnings from a 'non-pensionable' office or employment – a 'non-pensionable' employment is an employment where the employee is not a member of an employer-sponsored pension plan (i.e. not a member of an OPS).

Most self-employed individuals and individuals in non-pensionable employment have relevant earnings for pension contribution purposes.

'Net relevant earnings' are calculated by deducting allowable expenses and deductions, capital allowances and trading losses carried forward, from relevant earnings.

Note:

- Unused tax relief on personal pension contributions in any year can be carried forward to be offset against relevant earnings in subsequent years.
- Investment income (e.g. dividends, deposit income, rent) is **not** deemed to be relevant earnings for tax-allowable pension contribution purposes.

Claiming Personal Tax Relief on Pension Contributions

Self-employed individuals are obliged to file a personal income tax return each year. The deadline is 31 October (an extended deadline applies if the individual chooses to submit their tax return online). This deadline is relevant for:

- submitting an income tax return for the previous tax year (e.g. income tax returns for 2020 should be submitted by 31 October 2021);
- the payment of the balance of any taxes due for the previous year;
- the payment of preliminary tax for the current year (e.g. preliminary tax for 2021 should be paid by 31 October 2021);
- the payment of pension contributions and claiming personal tax relief on the contributions (at 20% or at 40%, as applicable) for the previous tax year.

'Preliminary tax' is the estimate of income tax/PAYE, PRSI and USC liabilities in a tax year. To avoid interest charges, preliminary tax should be calculated using one of the following options:

1. 90% of the tax due for that year; or
2. 100% of the tax due for the preceding year; or

3. 105% of the tax due for the pre-preceding year (this option only applies for direct debit tax payments and does not apply if the tax due for the pre-preceding year was nil).

The payment of personal pension contributions and the claiming of personal tax relief on the contributions (at 20% or at 40%, as applicable) for the previous tax year by the deadline of 31 October can result in:

- reducing or eliminating the balance of any tax due for the **previous** tax year; *and*
- reducing or eliminating the preliminary due for the **current** tax year.

EXAMPLE 3.3: BACKDATING PENSION CONTRIBUTIONS AND PRELIMINARY TAX

Mary is aged 33, is taxed as a single person and is self-employed. She has net relevant earnings of €60,000 for the previous tax year and is submitting her income tax return by 31 October.

Mary has a tax liability of €16,000 for the previous tax year, of which €12,000 has been paid; the balance of €4,000 is due. Mary's preliminary tax for the current year is based on 100% of the tax liability for the previous year.

Option 1

- Mary makes a tax payment of €20,000, i.e. a 'cash outflow' of €20,000.
- This tax payment consists of the tax balance of €4,000 due for the previous year + preliminary tax of €16,000 due for the current year (based on 100% of the tax liability for the previous year).

Option 2

- Mary makes a personal pension contribution of €10,000 and elects to claim personal tax relief on this contribution for the previous tax year.
- The tax relief on this contribution is €4,000 (i.e. pension contribution of €10,000 × 40%).
- The tax relief eliminates the tax balance due of €4,000 for the previous year.

- In addition, the preliminary tax is reduced to €12,000 for the current year (as based on 100% of the tax liability for the previous year, which has been reduced by €4,000 from €16,000 to €12,000).
- Mary's cash outflow is €22,000, i.e. a pension contribution of €10,000 + a preliminary tax payment of €12,000.

Accessing Retirement Benefits from a PPP or PRSA

Self-employed individuals can access retirement benefits between ages 60 and 75. (Earlier retirement and drawing on retirement benefits before age 60 is allowed for specific self-employed individuals, e.g. jockeys and fishermen.) In general, retirement benefits from a PPP or PRSA can be accessed by a combination of some or all of the options outlined in **Figure 3.3** below.

FIGURE 3.3: RETIREMENT BENEFITS FROM A PPP OR PRSA

To access retirement benefits from a PPP or a PRSA on retirement, a combination of some or all of the following options can apply			
1. Purchase an annuity	2. Take a lump sum	3. Invest in an approved retirement fund (ARF)	4. PRSA only: Remain invested in a PRSA
Use some or all of the pension plan value to purchase an annuity to provide a secure regular pension income for life.	Take a lump sum of up to 25% of the pension plan value, some or all of which can be paid tax free. The maximum combined tax-free lump sum from all pension plans is €200,000.	Reinvest some/all of capital accumulated in the pension plan in an ARF to provide income during retirement (subject to investing €63,500 in an approved minimum retirement fund (AMRF) until age 75, unless specific conditions are met).	After taking a lump sum, leave the remaining value of a PRSA plan invested in the PRSA (which becomes a 'vested PRSA') with the same treatment that applies to an ARF/AMRF.

In specific circumstances, after taking the initial tax-free lump sum as per **2** above, any remaining balance can be taken as a taxable lump sum.

Retirement benefit options are discussed in more detail in **Chapter 6**.

Retirement benefits can also be accessed from a PPP or a PRSA on the grounds of ill health, i.e. where an individual becomes permanently incapable of carrying out their own occupation, or a similar occupation, on the grounds of ill health.

In the event of death before retirement, the value of the PPP or PRSA is paid as a lump sum to the estate/beneficiaries of the PPP or PRSA holder. The beneficiaries may be subject to inheritance tax on the lump sum, depending on their relationship to the deceased PPP/PRSA holder.

Additional Pension Plan Options for Company Owners

The pension plan structures available to company owners who are in receipt of company-paid Schedule E income (as well as other employees) are generally the most flexible structures available in terms of contribution levels, investment choices and options for accessing benefits on retirement. These individuals have the option of an occupational pension scheme (OPS), in addition to a PPP or a PRSA.

The availability of flexible pension plan structures for company owners can be an important benefit of operating a business as a company, in addition to other benefits, such as limited liability and corporation tax rates. Company-paid contributions to an OPS are **not** subject to the tax-allowable limits that apply to personal pension contributions, in accordance with Revenue rules (as discussed in more detail later in this chapter).

In many cases, an OPS for a company owner is established as a 'one-member' pension plan, i.e. the only member of the plan is the company owner. These one-member OPS plans (often known as 'executive pension plans') are provided by the main life insurance companies and other providers.

A one-member OPS can provide a greater range of investment options compared to a group OPS for a group of employees (as discussed in **Chapter 4**), and provides greater confidentiality, as both the pension contributions paid to the pension plan for the company owner, and the pension plan value, would not be included in the annual report on a group OPS that would be available to all employees in the group OPS.

A one-member plan can also be established as a 'small self-administered scheme' that does not require the involvement of a life insurance company, and which provides the option of more control and direction over the investment of the pension contributions, including investment in direct assets, such as individual shares and property (for more information, see the "Self-administered/Self-directed Pension Plan Structures" section at the end of this chapter).

Occupational Pension Schemes

An OPS is the most common pension plan structure for company owners in receipt of company-paid Schedule E income and for employees in general, and is structured as a tax-exempt trust established by an employer for the purposes of providing retirement benefits and/or death benefits for individuals who are members of the OPS. The assets in the pension plan are held under trust and are thus legally separate from the employer's business assets. This separation can provide security for members and beneficiaries because, if the business fails, the pension plan is protected.

An OPS generally provides company owners with the option of making significant company-paid contributions to the pension plan that are allowable for corporation tax purposes **in addition** to contributions that can be personally paid by the owner that can be allowable for personal tax relief.

An OPS can also be established on a 'group' basis for a group of employees (see **Chapter 4**).

The normal retirement age (NRA) for members of an OPS is between 60 to 70 and early retirement is permitted from age 50 onwards, subject to conditions, as discussed in the "Accessing Retirement Benefits from an OPS" section below.

Establishing an Occupational Pension Scheme

An OPS is set up as follows:

- The company, i.e. the employer, establishes an OPS as a trust (a legal arrangement under which the investment assets are held, managed and controlled by a trustee).
- A Revenue-approved trust deed is executed to establish the OPS 'under trust'. In the case of a one-member plan (see above) with a life insurance company, a letter of exchange is used instead of a trust deed.
- The OPS must adopt a set of Revenue-approved rules, which address the practical, operational aspects of the OPS, such as eligibility criteria,

contribution levels and the maximum benefits to be provided. (Life insurance company plans normally adopt a standard set of rules that have been approved in advance by Revenue.)

- The nominated trustee can be the employer (i.e. the company). However, in practice, many employers appoint a third party to act as the trustee. Trustees are obliged to undergo appropriate trustee training on an ongoing basis. Where the company itself acts as the trustee, **all** of the company's directors are obliged to undergo trustee training. (See also **Chapter 4**.)
- At present, most OPS trust arrangements are set up as individual trusts. However, 'master trusts' may become the most common structure for employer-provided pension plans in Ireland due to the increasing regulatory requirements and costs for individual OPS trusts being implemented at an EU-wide level. A master trust is a multi-employer OPS under the governance of a single trustee board.
- The trustees of an OPS are obliged to appoint a registered administrator to undertake 'core administration functions' for the OPS, which include preparation of annual reports and annual member benefit statements on behalf of the trustees, maintenance of sufficient records to provide such services, and the submission of information to the Pensions Authority each year.
- The OPS is obliged to be registered with the Pensions Authority (typically arranged by the registered administrator) and an annual registration fee is payable.
- The trustees of an OPS are obliged to employ or enter into arrangements with advisors with qualifications and experience appropriate and relevant to the investment of the resources of the pension plan. In practice, this obligation is typically fulfilled by engaging an investment manager to invest the contributions paid into the OPS.

In the case of life insurance company plans (both one-member and group plans), a number of the above requirements are fulfilled by the life insurance company, i.e. the life insurance company: provides the trust deed/letter of exchange and the rules of the plan; arranges registration with the Pensions Authority and remits the annual fees; acts as the registered administrator; provides access to investment managers; and can arrange trustee training, if required.

OPS Contribution Levels

A condition of Revenue approval is that the employer must make a 'meaningful' contribution to an OPS. A 'meaningful' contribution is as follows:

- where the employer meets the initial and ongoing operating costs of the OPS and the costs of death-in-service cover; **or**
- where the employer pays at least one-tenth of the total ordinary annual contributions to the plan, exclusive of risk costs and employee additional voluntary contributions (i.e. for every €9 paid in by an employee, the employer must pay in at least €1).

For example, if an OPS has an employee contribution rate set at 4.5%, i.e. to join the OPS, the employee (including company owners) must make an ordinary contribution of 4.5%. In this case, the minimum 'meaningful' ordinary contribution by the employer is 0.5%, i.e. the total ordinary contributions amount to 5%, with the employer contribution equal to one-tenth of the total.

The employer is obliged to pay pension contributions (both employer and employee) to the trustees/pension plan provider within 21 days of the end of the month in which the pension contributions are due. This rule applies both to contributions to an OPS and to a group PRSA arranged by an employer (group PRSAs are discussed in **Chapter 4**).

The maximum pension contributions that can be paid to an OPS are determined by Revenue rules and formulae. A number of variables are relevant for the purposes of calculating the maximum contribution levels:

- salary/earnings from employment taxable under Schedule E, including taxable benefits-in-kind, such as employer-paid health insurance, company car, gym membership, etc.);
- normal retirement age (the stated NRA must be between age 60 and age 70; 65 is a commonly used NRA);
- potential length of service with the employer to normal retirement age;
- gender of the member;
- marital status of the member (i.e. single or married/civil partnership);
- value of existing pension plans from current employment (if any);
- value of any retained pension plan benefits from previous employments/occupations.

The contributions that can be paid to an OPS consist of 'ordinary annual contributions' and, if relevant, 'special contributions' can also be paid, as outlined below. (**Note**: these contribution options are relevant for all employees, not just company owners.)

Ordinary Annual Contributions

Two options are available for calculating the maximum ordinary (i.e. regular) annual contributions that can be paid in total into an OPS each year (i.e. employer and employee contributions combined), as shown in **Figure 3.4** below.

FIGURE **3.4**: OPTIONS FOR CALCULATING MAXIMUM ORDINARY ANNUAL CONTRIBUTIONS TO AN **OPS**

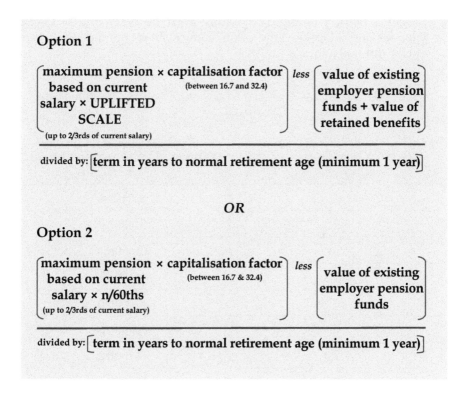

The **higher** result from the two options can be applied, and also note the following:

* under either option, the maximum allowable pension is 40/60ths (i.e. two-thirds) of salary;
* the capitalisation factors are provided by Revenue and are based on annuity rates in order to capitalise an annual pension, i.e. to calculate

the lump sum required to provide an annual pension (the capitalisation factors applicable at the time of writing are listed in **Figure 3.6** below);
- if the member is within three years of retirement, a current annuity rate can be used instead of the capitalisation factors listed in **Figure 3.6**, which can result in a higher maximum ordinary annual contribution, as annuity rates are very low at present;
- under Option 1, an **uplifted scale** from Revenue can be used in order to calculate the maximum allowable pension, as is shown in **Figure 3.5** below;
- under Option 1, the value of any retained pension benefits from previous employments/occupations **must** be taken into account, whereas under Option 2 the value of any such retained pension benefits is **not** taken into account.

FIGURE 3.5: REVENUE UPLIFTED SCALE FOR CALCULATING MAXIMUM PENSION

Years of service to normal retirement age	Expressed as a fraction of final remuneration
1	4/60ths
2	8/60ths
3	12/60ths
4	16/60ths
5	20/60ths
6	24/60ths
7	28/60ths
8	32/60ths
9	36/60ths
10 or more	40/60ths

Source: Revenue Pensions Manual: www.revenue.ie/en/tax-professionals/tdm/pensions/chapter-06.pdf

FIGURE 3.6: MAXIMUM BENEFIT CAPITALISATION FACTORS

Normal retirement age	Female, no spouse or civil partner	Female, with spouse or civil partner	Male, no spouse or civil partner	Male, with spouse or civil partner
60	27.5	30	24.4	32.4
61	26.8	29.2	23.6	31.6
62	26	28.4	22.8	30.8
63	25.3	27.5	22	30
64	24.6	26.7	21.2	29.2
65	23.8	25.9	20.4	28.4
66	23.1	25.1	19.6	27.6
67	22.4	24.3	18.9	26.8
68	21.6	23.5	18.1	26
69	20.9	22.6	17.4	25.2
70	20.2	21.8	16.7	24.4

Source: Revenue Pensions Manual: www.revenue.ie/en/tax-professionals/tdm/pensions/chapter-05.pdf

Example 3.4 below illustrates the application of the above calculation options.

EXAMPLE 3.4: CALCULATING ORDINARY ANNUAL CONTRIBUTIONS

John is married, aged 40, is a company owner, and is establishing an OPS. His salary is €60,000 and he has retained pension benefits from a previous employment valued at €50,000. John has been employed by his company for 1 year.

The NRA for the OPS is 65, so John has potentially 25 years of remaining service to his NRA.

Option 1

$$\left(\begin{array}{ccc}\text{John's current salary} \times \text{capitalisation factor} \\ \text{of €60,000} \times \text{uplifted} \quad \text{for married male} \\ \text{scale factor of} \qquad \text{with NRA of 65} \\ 40/60 \qquad = \\ = €40,000 \qquad 28.4\end{array}\right) \begin{array}{c} \textit{less} \end{array} \left(\begin{array}{c}\text{value of existing} \\ \text{employer pension} \\ \text{funds + value of} \\ \text{retained benefits} \\ = €50,000\end{array}\right)$$

$$\left[\begin{array}{c}\text{term in years to normal retirement date (minimum 1 year)} \\ = \text{25 years}\end{array}\right.$$

i.e. €40,000 × 28.4 = €1,136,000, less €50,000 = €1,086,000 / 25 years = €43,440.

Under Option 1, the maximum annual contribution is **€43,440**.

Option 2

$$\left(\begin{array}{ccc}\text{John's current salary} \times \text{capitalisation factor} \\ \text{of €60,000} \times \qquad \text{for married male} \\ \text{factor of} \qquad \text{with NRA of 65} \\ 25/60 \qquad = \\ = €25,000 \qquad 28.4\end{array}\right) \begin{array}{c} \textit{less} \end{array} \left(\begin{array}{c}\text{value of} \\ \text{existing} \\ \text{employer} \\ \text{pension funds} \\ = \text{nil}\end{array}\right)$$

$$\left[\begin{array}{c}\text{term in years to normal retirement date (minimum 1 year)} \\ = \text{25 years}\end{array}\right.$$

i.e. €25,000 × 28.4 = €710,000 / 25 years = €28,400.

Under Option 2, the maximum annual contribution is **€28,400**.

The **higher** result from the two options can be used, so the maximum allowable annual contribution is €43,440.

Note: the maximum annual contribution is the maximum for the **combined** employer and employee contribution levels. Employee contributions are subject to limits, similar to self-employed individuals, based on age-related percentages of annual earnings (subject to an annual earnings cap of €115,000), as per the table in **Figure 3.2**. Employer contributions are **not** subject to these limits.

In **Example 3.4** above, John is 40, so, based on Revenue rules, he can contribute up to 25% of his gross annual earnings into his pension and avail of tax relief on that contribution. Therefore, his annual employee contribution level is €15,000 (€60,000 × 25%). *Note*: the employer contribution level is **not** subject to such limits, provided that the combined employee and employer contribution level does not exceed the maximum allowable amount of €43,440 as calculated under Option 1.

The above calculations refer the maximum ordinary (i.e. regular) contributions that can be paid into an OPS each year. Regular contributions are typically paid monthly or annually.

Regular contributions paid by an employer are allowable for business tax relief (i.e. income tax or corporation tax) during the period in which the contributions have been paid. *Note*: accrued contributions in the business accounts at the end of a taxable period are **not** allowable for business tax relief in that period – the contributions must have been paid within that taxable period.

Revenue has issued a table of maximum contribution rates as a percentage of salary, based on the above calculations. This table is shown in **Figure 3.7** below (reproduced with the permission of New Ireland Assurance) and is based on the following assumptions:

- the maximum contribution rate must include both employer and employee contributions but exclude the cost of death-in-service cover, i.e. the maximum contribution does not have to be reduced if the employer also pays for death-in-service cover as part of the OPS;
- these contribution rates assume that the individual does **not** have any existing pension benefits and that they will have completed **at least 10 years' service** at NRA; and
- the rates shown for individuals within three years to retirement are based on indicative annuity rates and are subject to change. Annuity rates are based on 3.5% escalation, 10-year guarantee period with no overlap and 100% of an individual's pension will go to their spouse for the remainder of that spouse's life. In practice, if the individual is within three years of their NRA, a specific calculation should be undertaken using annuity rates specific to their circumstances, i.e. exact date of birth for the individual and their spouse (if any), personal health issues, etc.

FIGURE 3.7: MAXIMUM CONTRIBUTION RATES

Age	NRA 60				NRA 65				NRA 70			
	Male Single	Male Married	Female Single	Female Married	Male Single	Male Married	Female Single	Female Married	Male Single	Male Married	Female Single	Female Married
19	40%	53%	45%	49%	30%	41%	35%	38%	22%	32%	26%	29%
20	41%	54%	46%	50%	30%	42%	35%	38%	22%	33%	27%	29%
21	42%	55%	47%	51%	31%	43%	36%	39%	23%	33%	28%	30%
22	43%	57%	48%	53%	32%	44%	37%	40%	23%	34%	28%	30%
23	44%	58%	50%	54%	32%	45%	38%	41%	24%	35%	29%	31%
24	45%	60%	51%	56%	33%	46%	39%	42%	24%	35%	29%	32%
25	47%	62%	52%	57%	34%	47%	40%	43%	25%	36%	30%	32%
26	48%	64%	54%	59%	35%	49%	41%	44%	25%	37%	31%	33%
27	49%	66%	56%	61%	36%	50%	42%	45%	26%	38%	31%	34%
28	51%	68%	57%	63%	37%	51%	43%	47%	27%	39%	32%	35%
29	53%	70%	59%	65%	38%	53%	44%	48%	27%	40%	33%	35%
30	54%	72%	61%	67%	39%	54%	45%	49%	28%	41%	34%	36%
31	56%	75%	63%	69%	40%	56%	47%	51%	29%	42%	35%	37%
32	58%	77%	66%	71%	41%	57%	48%	52%	29%	43%	35%	38%
33	60%	80%	68%	74%	43%	59%	50%	54%	30%	44%	36%	39%
34	63%	83%	71%	77%	44%	61%	51%	56%	31%	45%	37%	40%
35	65%	86%	73%	80%	45%	63%	53%	58%	32%	47%	39%	42%
36	68%	90%	76%	83%	47%	65%	55%	60%	33%	48%	40%	43%
37	71%	94%	80%	87%	49%	68%	57%	62%	34%	49%	41%	44%
38	74%	98%	83%	91%	50%	70%	59%	64%	35%	51%	42%	45%
39	78%	103%	87%	95%	52%	73%	61%	66%	36%	53%	43%	47%
40	81%	108%	92%	100%	54%	76%	64%	69%	37%	54%	45%	48%
41	86%	114%	97%	105%	57%	79%	66%	72%	38%	56%	46%	50%
42	90%	120%	102%	111%	59%	82%	69%	75%	40%	58%	48%	52%
43	96%	127%	108%	118%	62%	86%	72%	79%	41%	60%	50%	54%
44	102%	135%	115%	125%	65%	90%	76%	82%	43%	63%	52%	56%
45	109%	144%	122%	133%	68%	95%	79%	86%	45%	65%	54%	58%
46	116%	154%	131%	143%	72%	100%	84%	91%	46%	68%	56%	61%
47	125%	166%	141%	154%	76%	105%	88%	96%	48%	71%	59%	63%
48	136%	180%	153%	167%	80%	111%	93%	102%	51%	74%	61%	66%
49	148%	196%	167%	182%	85%	118%	99%	108%	53%	78%	64%	69%
50	163%	216%	183%	200%	91%	126%	106%	115%	56%	81%	67%	73%
51	181%	240%	204%	222%	97%	135%	113%	123%	59%	86%	71%	77%
52	203%	270%	229%	250%	105%	146%	122%	133%	62%	90%	75%	81%

53	233%	309%	262%	286%	113%	158%	132%	144%	66%	96%	79%	86%
54	271%	360%	306%	333%	124%	172%	144%	157%	70%	102%	84%	91%
55	311%	414%	351%	383%	136%	189%	159%	173%	74%	109%	90%	97%
56	390%	517%	439%	479%	151%	210%	176%	192%	80%	116%	96%	104%
57	755%	1004%	819%	906%	170%	237%	198%	216%	86%	125%	104%	112%
58	1093%	1464%	1187%	1319%	194%	271%	227%	247%	93%	136%	112%	121%
59	2106%	2836%	2295%	2542%	227%	316%	265%	288%	101%	148%	123%	132%
60					260%	363%	304%	331%	111%	163%	135%	145%
61					326%	453%	380%	413%	124%	181%	150%	162%
62					633%	858%	689%	768%	139%	203%	168%	182%
63					915%	1247%	1004%	1112%	159%	233%	192%	208%
64					1758%	2399%	1916%	2141%	186%	271%	225%	242%
65									213%	311%	258%	278%
66									267%	390%	322%	348%
67									523%	721%	568%	635%
68									751%	1043%	819%	915%
69									1437%	2000%	1568%	1753%
70												

Source: The Revenue Commissioners

Special Contributions

In addition to paying ordinary annual contributions, an employer may also be in a position to make special contributions to an OPS in order to provide retirement benefits for an employee's past service. 'Past service' in this context refers to years of employment with the same employer during which little or no pension contributions were paid. For example, an employer may wish to make a top-up pension contribution payment for a long-serving employee, or a company owner employed by the company may wish to arrange for the company to make a top-up pension contribution for the owner, say to cover the early years of the company when no pension contributions were paid.

In order to calculate if scope exists to make a special contribution, the employer/professional advisor should:

- calculate the maximum fund value that the individual could have if the individual left service today based on an early retirement funding calculation (as shown below);
- deduct the value of pension benefits currently in place, including any retained benefits from previous employments/self-employments.

Unlike the ordinary annual contribution calculation options as shown in **Figure 3.4** above, Revenue does not provide specific guidance on the calculation methodology for special contributions. In the absence of such guidance, many pension plan providers, such as life insurance companies, use the following methodology:

- **Step 1:** calculate the Revenue maximum pension based on years of service with the employer to date using the following 'early retirement' calculation:

$$\frac{\text{Actual years of service at early retirement age (i.e. to date)}}{\text{Potential years of service to normal retirement age}} \times \frac{\text{Maximum annual pension at normal retirement age}}{}$$

- **Step 2:** Calculate the maximum special contribution allowed by multiplying the maximum annual pension calculated in Step 1 by the relevant capitalisation factor provided by Revenue, as listed in **Figure 3.6** above (as with the calculation of the ordinary annual contribution, current annuity rates can be used instead where the individual is within three years of normal retirement age).

Example 3.5 demonstrates the application of this methodology.

EXAMPLE 3.5: CALCULATING A SPECIAL PENSION CONTRIBUTION

Yvonne established her business two years ago as a limited company. The company is establishing a one-member OPS for Yvonne's benefit with a normal retirement age of 65. Yvonne is single, aged 45 and does not have retained pension benefits from previous employments/self-employments. She is currently withdrawing a gross annual salary of €35,000. Yvonne wants to calculate the maximum special pension contribution payable to the OPS, and Yvonne also wishes to calculate the maximum ordinary pension contribution that can be paid, if a special contribution is paid.

Step 1: calculate the Revenue maximum pension based on years of service with the employer to date using the 'early retirement' calculation as follows:

The early retirement calculation is:

$$\frac{\text{actual years of service to date}}{\text{potential years to NRA}} \times \frac{\text{maximum pension}}{\text{at NRA}}$$

Yvonne's actual service to date is two years and potential service to normal retirement age is 22 years; therefore, the maximum pension is calculated as:

$$\frac{2 \text{ years}}{22 \text{ years}} \times \begin{array}{c}(\text{Yvonne's salary of €35,000} \times \\ \text{uplifted scale factor of } 40/60)\end{array} = \text{€2,121 p.a.}$$

Step 2: Calculate the maximum special contribution allowed by multiplying the maximum pension (as calculated above) by the applicable capitalisation factor as per the Revenue table of capitalisation factors in **Figure 3.6**. The calculation is:

$$\begin{array}{c}\text{maximum pension} \\ \text{of €2,121 p.a.}\end{array} \times \begin{array}{c}\text{capitalisation} \\ \text{factor of 23.8}\end{array} = \text{€50,480}$$

Therefore, Yvonne's company can make a special contribution payment of €50,480 to the OPS.

Step 3: Calculate the maximum ordinary annual contribution allowed, assuming the above special contribution is made, in this case:

$$\frac{\text{(Yvonne's salary } \times \text{ uplifted scale factor)} \times \text{capitalisation factor} - \text{special contribution}}{\text{term from now to NRA}}$$

Which, in this case is:

$$\frac{\left(\text{€35,000} \times \dfrac{40}{60}\right) \times 23.8 - \text{€50,480}}{20 \text{ years}} = \text{€25,242}$$

The maximum ordinary annual contribution allowed is therefore €25,242.

Step 4: The maximum pension contribution that Yvonne's limited company can pay to the OPS is €75,722, i.e.:

$$\text{special contribution of €50,480 (Step 2)} + \text{maximum ordinary annual contribution of €25,242 (Step 3)} = \text{€75,722}$$

Business tax relief is allowable on special contributions in the period in which the special contribution is actually paid, provided that the amount of the special contribution does not exceed the greater of €6,350 or the amount of regular contributions paid during the same period.

If the amount of the special contribution exceeds the greater of €6,350 or the amount of regular contributions paid during the same period, then:

- the business tax relief on the special contribution is spread over a number of years;
- the number of years is calculated by dividing the amount of the special contribution by the amount of the regular contributions, subject to a maximum spread of five years and a minimum divisor of €6,350.

In **Example 3.5** above, as €25,242 is the maximum ordinary annual contribution, the amount of the special contribution of €50,480 that would qualify for business tax relief in the current year would be limited to €25,242 with the balance of €25,238 carried forward to the following year for business tax relief purposes, i.e.:

$$\frac{\text{special contribution}}{\text{maximum regular contribution}} = \frac{\text{€50,480}}{\text{€25,242}} = 2 \text{ (years)}$$

Therefore, the special contribution of €50,480 must be spread over two years for business tax relief purposes, as the special contribution is twice the maximum regular contribution.

Accessing Retirement Benefits from an OPS

The normal retirement age for accessing retirement benefits from an OPS is between 60 and 70.

Retirement benefits can be taken at the normal retirement age **without** the OPS member having to cease employment or dispose of their shareholding. No maximum age exists for taking retirement benefits from an OPS.

Retirement benefits from an OPS can be accessed by a combination of some, or all, of the options outlined in **Figure 3.8**.

FIGURE 3.8: ACCESSING RETIREMENT BENEFITS FROM AN OPS

To access retirement benefits from an OPS on retirement, a combination of some or all of the following options can apply		
1. Purchase an annuity	**2. Take a lump sum**	**3. Invest in an ARF**
Use some or all of the pension plan value to purchase an annuity to provide a secure regular pension income for life.	Allowable lump sum (some or all of the lump sum can be paid tax-free), calculated as: • up to 25% of the pension plan value; or • can be based on a multiple of salary for an OPS – up to 1.5 times salary. The maximum combined tax-free lump sum from all pension plans is €200,000.	Reinvest some/all of capital accumulated in the pension plan in an ARF in order to provide income during retirement, subject to investing €63,500 in an approved minimum retirement fund (AMRF) until age 75, unless specific conditions are met.

In specific circumstances, after taking the initial lump sum as per Option 2 above, any remaining balance can be taken as a taxable lump sum.

Retirement benefits from an OPS (as per **Figure 3.8**) can also be accessed before normal retirement age from age 50 onwards, known as taking benefits on 'early retirement'. To access early retirement benefits, the following conditions are required:

• the OPS member must be aged 50 or over; and
• the member must have ceased employment with that employer and in the case of a 20% director (i.e. an individual who directly or indirectly owns or controls more than 20% of the voting rights in the employer company at any time in the three-year period prior to early retirement), the individual must dispose of their shareholding and sever all links with the company before early retirement benefits can be taken.

Note: the OPS member can continue to work as an employee with another employer, or as a self-employed individual. Taking early retirement from an OPS does not preclude the individual from continuing to work elsewhere.

Retirement benefit options are discussed in more detail in **Chapter 6**.

Ill-health and Death Benefits from an OPS

Retirement benefits from an OPS can be taken at any time on the grounds of ill health. 'Ill health' refers to physical or mental deterioration (as diagnosed by a medical professional), which is serious enough to prevent the OPS member from following normal employment or which seriously impairs their earning capacity. *Note:* this definition of ill health is far **less** stringent than the definition of ill health under a PPP or PRSA (see the section on "Accessing Retirement Benefits from a PPP or PRSA" above).

In the event of the pension plan member dying before normal retirement, the value in the OPS is used to provide benefits to dependants, typically a lump sum, with any balance used to provide a dependant's pension. A spouse or civil partner is automatically deemed to be a dependant and children are normally dependants until they reach the age of 18 (or 21 if in full-time education).

A separate life cover policy can also be arranged by the employer to provide life cover for the member, known as 'death-in-service cover', to provide a lump sum payable in the event of his or her death. The employer can also arrange income protection/disability cover for the member to provide an ongoing income in the event of illness or injury. This insurance can be arranged on a 'one-person' basis, e.g. for an individual company owner who is employed by the company, or on a 'group' basis, i.e. for a group of employees (which can include the company owner who is employed by the company).

The ongoing costs of the life cover policy paid by the employer are allowable for business tax relief in the same manner as employer pension contributions. The ongoing costs of employer-paid income protection/disability cover are also allowed for business tax relief. (See **Chapter 5** for more information.)

Under Revenue rules, the maximum lump sum payable on death prior to retirement is four times final salary, plus an amount equal to the return of the value of the deceased member's own contributions (including AVCs, if any). Any balance in the OPS would then be used to provide a dependant's pension, by purchasing an annuity.

Pension Plan Transfers

Permitted transfers between pension plans are summarised in **Figure 3.9** below:

FIGURE 3.9: SUMMARY OF TRANSFERS BETWEEN PENSION PLANS

To: From:	PRSA	PPP	OPS	PRB *(Personal Retirement Bond)*	Overseas Plan
PRSA	YES	NO	YES	NO	YES[1, 5]
PPP	YES	YES	NO[2]	NO	NO[3]
OPS	YES[4]	NO	YES	YES	YES[1]
PRB	NO	NO	YES	YES	YES[1]
Overseas Plan	YES	YES	YES	YES	

Notes:
[1] Provided the receiving overseas plan meets specific requirements.
[2] A PPP can transfer to a PRSA, which can then transfer to an OPS.
[3] A PPP can transfer to a PRSA, which can then transfer to an overseas plan, provided the receiving plan meets specific requirements.
[4] Some restrictions apply.
[5] Income tax applies to the amount transferred from a PRSA to an overseas pension.
Source: with the permission of Irish Life.

The options for OPS members when changing employment are discussed further in **Chapter 4** in the section on "Options for OPS Members when Leaving an Employment".

Self-administered/Self-directed Pension Plan Structures

Pension plans can be structured as 'self-administered' or 'self-directed' arrangements in order to enable investment in direct investment assets, such as individual shares, property, bonds, deposits, etc., in addition to investing in pooled investment funds.

In many cases, these arrangements are used by company owners (and by employees in one-member plans) and by self-employed individuals who wish to have the option of more control and direction over the investment of the funds in the pension plan. A number of self-administered/self-directed arrangements are available, including:

1. **Small Self-administered Scheme (SSAS)**: structured as an OPS (usually a one-member plan) without the involvement of a life insurance company, this structure is used mainly by company owners employed by the company (but can also be used by other employees). Revenue requires that a 'pensioneer trustee' must be appointed as a trustee to a SSAS, to assist with ensuring that the SSAS operates within Revenue rules. Revenue-approved pensioneer trustees are individuals or corporate bodies with specialist knowledge and experience in the area of SSASs and pensions in general. The Association of Pension Trustees of Ireland is a representative body for pensioneer trustees and provides a list of members who are Revenue-approved pensioneer trustees (see www.apti.ie).

2. **Executive Pension Plan – Self-directed Option:** a one-member executive pension plan, provided by life insurance companies, and other providers, and structured as an OPS. These plans are available for company owners employed by the company and for other employees, and provide an underlying 'self-directed' option to enable investment in direct assets such as individual shares and property.

3. **PPP – Self-directed Option:** a PPP provided by a life insurance company – available for self-employed individuals and individuals in non-pensionable employment– that provides an underlying 'self-directed' option to enable investment in direct assets, such as individual shares and property.

4. **Self-directed PRSA:** a PRSA structure available through specialist providers to enable the funds in a PRSA to be invested in direct assets.

5. **Self-directed Personal Retirement Bond (PRB):** a PRB structure available through specialist providers to enable the funds in the PRB to be invested in direct assets.

6. **Self-directed Approved (Minimum) Retirement Fund (A(M)RF):** an A(M)RF structure available through specialist providers to enable funds to be invested in direct assets.

Investments by Self-administered/Self-directed Pension Plan Structures

All investment undertaken by self-administered/self-directed pension plan structures must be on an arm's length basis (i.e. where both parties to the investment transaction act independently without one party influencing the other) and a number of restrictions apply to invest-ments, including:

1. **Loans** Loans are prohibited by the self-administered structure to pension plan members to any other individual having a contingent interest in the pension plan, or to the employer.
2. **Investment Property** When acquiring a property, the seller must be at arm's length from the pension plan and the employer, including directors and associated companies. The purpose of the acquisition must be for long-term investment purposes and not for disposal or letting to the employer, including its directors and associated com-panies. Similarly, a sale of a property by the pension plan must be on an arm's length basis. Property development is not permitted. Borrowing to fund the purchase of property is permitted.
3. **Self-investment** The pension plan cannot purchase property or other fixed assets from the employer and cannot purchase shares in the employer company.
4. **'Pride in Possession Articles'** Investment in personal chattels, including works of art, jewellery, vintage cars, yachts, etc., is not permitted.
5. **Private Companies** Investment in private companies must be limited to 5% of the pension plan's assets and to 10% of the private company's share capital.

10 Key Points: Pension Planning For Sole Traders, Partners and Company Owners

1. Pension planning is a very important method of extracting some of the income generated by a business in order to provide retirement benefits for the business owner.
2. Two types of pension plan structures are available for self-employed business owners, i.e. a personal pension plan (PPP) and a personal retirement savings account (PRSA). Personal income tax relief is granted on personal contributions paid into these plans, subject to age-related percentage limits, and pen-sion contributions can be backdated to the previous year for tax relief purposes (subject to conditions).
3. In addition to the above options, a company can establish an occupational pension scheme (OPS) for the benefit of a com-pany owner who is in receipt of company-paid income tax-able under Schedule E. An OPS can also be established for all employees (i.e. not just a company owner).

4. These pension plans (i.e. PPP, PRSA and OPS) can also provide benefits in the event of death or ill health.

5. An OPS is a tax-exempt trust established by an employer for the purposes of providing retirement benefits and/or death benefits for employees. Pension plan assets held under trust are legally separate from the employer's business assets, which can provide security for pension plan members and beneficiaries.

6. In many cases, an OPS for a company owner is established as a 'one-member' pension plan, i.e. the only member of the plan is the company owner.

7. The maximum pension contributions that can be paid to an OPS are determined by Revenue rules and formulae. Depending on the age of the company owner/employee and other factors, contributions in excess of 100% of annual salary can be paid into an OPS each year in specific circumstances.

8. In addition to ongoing contributions, special contributions to an OPS can also be paid, in order to provide retirement benefits for a company owner/employee's past service. 'Past service' in this context refers to years of employment with the same employer during which little or no pension contributions were paid.

9. The normal retirement age for members of an OPS is age 60 to 70. Accessing benefits before normal retirement age (NRA), known as taking benefits on 'early retirement', is permitted from age 50 onwards, provided that the member (i.e. the company owner/employee) has ceased employment with the employer and severed all links with the employer. The OPS member can continue to work as an employee with another employer, or as a self-employed individual; taking early retirement from an OPS does not preclude the individual from continuing to work elsewhere.

10. Pension plans can be structured as 'self-administered/self-directed' arrangements in order to enable investment in direct investment assets, such as individual shares, property, bonds, deposits, etc., subject to restrictions, in addition to investing in pooled investment funds.

4.

Employee Pension and Life Insurance Plans

- Introduction
- Overview of Pension Plans Provided for Employees
- Employers and Group Occupational Pension Schemes
- PRSA Plans on a 'Group' Basis
- Additional Voluntary Contributions (AVCs)
- Options for OPS Members when Leaving an Employment
- Redundancy Payments and Pension Plans
- Life Insurance for Employees
- Examples of Employee Pension Plan and Life Insurance Benefits in Practice

Introduction

An employer-sponsored pension plan is a valuable benefit for employees. For many employees, pension plan benefits built up during employment will be their most important financial asset in retirement.

As well as salary, other employee benefits are often cited by employees as a key factor in accepting a job offer. Core employee benefits typically include a pension plan, health insurance and life insurance, such as death-in-service cover and income protection/disability cover. Such benefits have become increasingly important for hiring and retaining staff, particularly for employers in sectors where demand for skilled people is high, such as export-orientated technology and financial services sectors, and particularly for senior employees, who tend to be older and more likely to place a much higher value on pension and insurance benefits, compared to more junior, younger employees.

Chapter 3 focuses on 'one-person' pension plan options for self-employed business owners, including the PRSA structure and the OPS structure. This chapter focuses on options for groups of employees (i.e. more than one person), consisting of a group OPS and a group PRSA.

The following topics are covered in this chapter:

- overview of pension plans provided for employees;
- employers and group occupational pension schemes;
- PRSA plans on a 'group' basis;
- additional voluntary contributions (AVCs);
- options for OPS members when leaving an employment;
- redundancy payments and pension plans;
- life insurance for employees;
- examples of employee pension plan and life insurance benefits in practice.

Overview of Pension Plans Provided for Employees

Pension plans provided by employers for employees are typically provided on a group basis and are structured as:

- occupational pension scheme (OPS); and/or
- personal retirement savings account (PRSA).

FIGURE **4.1**: GROUP PENSION PLANS FOR EMPLOYEES

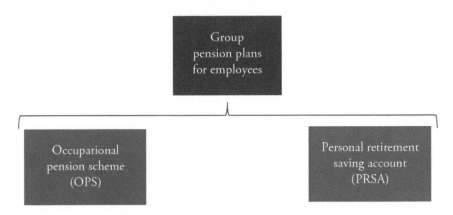

Many employers make an employer contribution to a pension plan that they have set up for their employees. This contribution is typically expressed as a percentage of the employee's salary. Typical employer and employee pension contribution percentages are in a range of 3% to 10% of salary (or higher in some cases), and are often paid on a 'matching basis', whereby the employer will make a matching contribution (up to a maximum level) on the basis that the employee makes a matching contribution.

Large, stable and well-established employers are likely to make higher employer contributions when compared with smaller, more recently established employers at the early stages of growing and developing their businesses.

Some employers make a contribution based on the employee contribution up to a specific level; some employers have a flat contribution rate; and some employers operate eligibility criteria for employees wishing to join the pension plan (such as a waiting period of up to six months).

Employers may also provide different pension plans for different categories of employee, for example, a separate pension plan can be provided for senior management into which the employer may decide to make higher contributions than are paid into the pension plan for the general workforce, and/or 'one-member' pension plans can be provided for individual employees. (One-member (i.e. one-person) plans are discussed in **Chapter 3**.)

Employers often engage the services of an independent advisor/broker in order to advise on and assist with the selection, establishment and ongoing operation of appropriate pension plans, including the provision of advice and services to employees (employee briefing sessions, enrolment for joiners, options for leavers, annual reviews, investment strategy advice, etc.).

Employers and Group Occupational Pension Schemes

The steps required to establish an OPS are set out in **Chapter 3** in the section on "Establishing an Occupational Pension Scheme". A 'group' OPS is an OPS for a group of employees (rather than for just one employee).

As covered in **Chapter 3**, an OPS is a tax-exempt trust established by an employer for the purposes of providing retirement benefits and/or death benefits for employees. In the past, the employer often acted as the trustee of the pension plan; however, in recent times employers have been appointing third parties to act as trustee, due to the legal duties and responsibilities of trustees, and the requirement for ongoing appropriate trustee training. (All existing trustees are required to undergo appropriate trustee training every two years and new trustees are required to undergo appropriate trustee training within six months of their appointment. As mentioned in **Chapter 3**, where the employer company is acting as the trustee, **all** directors, including non-executive directors and/or non-resident directors, are required to undergo appropriate trustee training.)

The trustees of an OPS are obliged to appoint a registered administrator to undertake core administration functions for the pension plan. The trustees of an OPS are also obliged to employ or enter into arrangements with advisors with qualifications and experience appropriate and relevant to the investment of the resources of the plan. (See also **Chapter 3**.)

In practice, most group pension plans are provided through life insurance companies and other large financial services providers, which can resource a number of the functions required, i.e. trustee, registered administrator and investment manager functions.

As set out in **Chapter 3** in the section on "OPS Contribution Levels", the employer is obliged to make a 'meaningful' contribution to an OPS.

The employer is also obliged to pay pension contributions (both employer and employee) to the trustees/pension plan provider within 21 days of the end of the month in which the pension contributions are due or are deducted from employees. This rule applies both to contributions to an OPS and to a PRSA that has been arranged by an employer.

Trustees are obliged to provide the employer and pension plan members (i.e. the employees in the pension plan) with ongoing information within specified timeframes, as follows:

- **Annual Benefit Statement and Statement of Reasonable Projection** – to be provided to members each year. The information contained in these documents should relate to a date no earlier than six months from the date the documents are given to members.
- **Trustee Annual Report** – to be issued within nine months of the pension plan year end and to be made available to members and other relevant parties, such as authorised trade unions of which the employees are members.

The key components of a group OPS are shown in **Figure 4.2** below.

FIGURE 4.2: KEY COMPONENTS OF A GROUP OCCUPATIONAL PENSION SCHEME

Meaningful contribution and 21-day rule — Employer

Advisor — Advises on and coordinates set up and ongoing operation

Trustees — Legal duties and responsibilities and ongoing training required

Group occupational pension scheme

Members (employees) — Receive ongoing scheme information

Registered administrator — Provides core administration functions

Investment manager — Invests the contributions and manages the assets

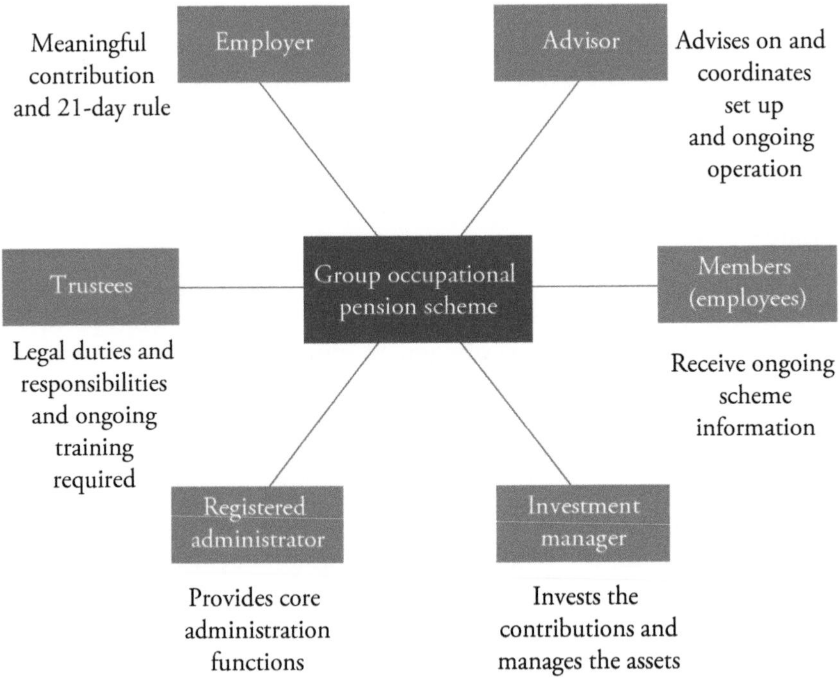

PRSA Plans on a 'Group' Basis

At the time of writing, employers **are not** legally obliged to contribute to a pension plan for the benefit of their employees, although plans for employee automatic enrolment in pension plans in the coming years will likely result in mandatory employer pension contributions (see **Chapter 1**). However, employers **are** legally obliged to provide employees with access to a pension plan. The minimum requirement is the provision of access to a standard PRSA (see the section on "Personal Retirement Savings Accounts (PRSAs)" in **Chapter 3**).

A 'group' PRSA plan is an arrangement facilitated by an employer whereby employees can establish a PRSA in their own names as part of a group arrangement (i.e. an arrangement that covers a group of employees). The employer remits employee contributions (and employer contributions, if relevant) to the PRSA provider. The employer is obliged to deduct employee contributions from employee gross pay and adjust employee payroll taxes to take account of the relevant employee income tax relief.

A trustee is not required for a PRSA and employees select the investment funds available from the PRSA provider in which to invest their contributions. Accordingly, PRSA plans can sometimes be viewed as less onerous and less costly from an employer perspective.

However, a PRSA can be viewed as less attractive than an OPS for employees (and for employers in some cases) for the following reasons:

- **Higher costs** Annual management charges for a PRSA typically start at 1%. The annual management charge for an OPS (which is deducted from the employee pension plan value) can be reduced if the employer separately pays for the administration costs, regulatory fees and advisor fees.
- **Fewer options for employees on retirement** Compared to a PRSA, an OPS provides a greater range of options for taking benefits on retirement (see **Chapter 6**).
- **Lower tax-allowable contributions for employees** For employees who wish to make significant employee contributions to the pension plan, to which employer contributions are also paid, a higher level of employee contributions can qualify for tax relief in the case of an OPS compared to a PRSA.

- **Costs or restrictions on transferring benefits from other pension plans** Employees who wish to transfer pension plan values from previous employments may be subject to costs and restrictions if transferring into a PRSA. Costs or restrictions should **not** apply to similar transfers into an OPS.
- **Taxes on transfers overseas** PRSA transfers overseas incur a tax charge equal to the employee's marginal rate of tax. This tax charge does **not** apply to OPS transfers overseas.
- **No refund of the value of contributions** If an employee leaves employment within two years of joining an OPS, the employer can elect to receive a refund of the employer contributions that have been paid into the employee's plan, and the employee would receive a refund of the value of their contributions to the pension plan (less tax at 20%). This refund option is **not** available for a PRSA.
- **No death/illness cover benefits** A PRSA structure can only be used for pension plan purposes, and death and/or illness cover benefits cannot be provided by a PRSA. A separate plan or policy would need to be established by the employer to provide death and/or illness cover benefits for employees, whereas an OPS can provide these benefits alongside the pension plan within the one structure. (See the section on "Life Insurance for Employees" later in this chapter.)

Additional Voluntary Contributions (AVCs)

Employees in an OPS have the option to make additional voluntary contributions (AVCs). The reasons for making AVCs are as follows:

- the levels of basic employer/employee contributions paid into many pension plans may not be sufficient to provide adequate pension income in retirement;
- the levels of basic employer/employee contributions (often paid on a matching basis) are typically calculated on base annual salary and are typically not adjusted to take account of other taxable emoluments such as bonuses or benefits-in-kind.

AVCs can be paid to:

- the main employer OPS;
- a separate group AVC plan (see below);
- an AVC PRSA (see below).

In the event of the death of an employee before retirement, the value of any employee AVC funds is typically paid as a lump sum to the beneficiaries of the deceased.

Public sector workers (who are members of a public sector superannuation pension scheme) who have, or will have, less than the maximum 40 years' service at retirement, may have the option to make additional contributions to 'purchase' additional years of service that can be counted in determining their pension benefits payable at retirement.

Tax Relief

In order to calculate the scope for income tax relief, an employee's AVCs need to be added to their contributions to the main OPS. The overall contribution limits for employees (i.e. limits for employee contributions to the main OPS and for AVCs combined) are based on age-related percentages of annual gross earning as per the table in **Figure 4.3** below. The maximum limits apply to annual gross earnings up to €115,000 – earnings above this earnings cap of €115,000 cannot be included.

FIGURE **4.3**: EMPLOYEE AGE-RELATED PERCENTAGE LIMITS FOR TAX RELIEF

Age	Contribution Limits for Tax Relief (% of remuneration)
Under 30	15%
30 to 39	20%
40 to 49	25%
50 to 54	30%
55 to 59	35%
60+	40%

(*Note:* the above limits are identical to the limits that apply for self-employed personal contributions, as discussed in **Chapter 3**.)

Employees in an OPS, who were in the same employment in the previous year, have the option of making an AVC to the OPS and backdating the tax relief to the previous year, i.e. claiming a refund of PAYE from the previous year. A PAYE refund from the previous year is subject to the overall limits in the table in **Figure 4.3** above that were applicable during the previous year. The deadline for making an AVC payment and backdating the tax relief is the 31 October in the current year (an extended deadline applies if the employee submits a tax return online).

Note: the payment of an AVC to be backdated to the previous year for tax relief cannot be paid via salary deduction (as would the case for regular employee contributions, typically paid monthly). The employee would need to personally make the AVC payment to the OPS, and would then need to personally arrange to claim the PAYE refund from Revenue.

AVC PRSAs

An AVC PRSA is a PRSA arrangement established by an individual employee in their own name, without the involvement of their employer. An AVC PRSA can provide more flexibility as the employee can have a different advisor for the AVC PRSA (rather than dealing only with the advisor to the main employer pension plan), and the employee can select the investment manager(s) and investment funds (rather than just investing in the funds provided under the main employer plan or under a separate group AVC plan).

The charges for an AVC PRSA can sometimes be higher than the charges that apply to the main employer plan or to a separate group AVC plan.

Options for OPS Members when Leaving an Employment

Employees who are members of an OPS have a number of options on leaving employment regarding the value of their benefit in the OPS:

1. Take a refund of their own contributions/value of their own contributions (including AVCs, if any). However:

   - This option is only available if the employee has **less** than two years' 'qualifying service' – under this option employees are **not** entitled to the value of the employer contributions.

     'Qualifying service' is the aggregate of each period of 'reckonable service', i.e. service in the relevant employment while a member of the pension plan(s).

   - The pension plan(s) consist of the current plan, every other plan relating to the same employment **and** a previous employer's plan where the benefits of that plan (if that previous plan was an OPS) have been **transferred to the current plan**.

2. Leave the benefit in the current plan, i.e. the benefit becomes deferred or paid-up, whereby the employee is a deferred member of the plan. The benefit remains invested in the plan (unless the plan is winding up) until the employee decides otherwise by accessing benefits on retirement or transferring the value of the benefit to another plan.

3. Transfer the value of the contributions, including AVCs, if any, into a PRSA (if the employee has 15 years or less service in the OPS). A 'certificate of benefit comparison' can be required if the transfer value is greater than €10,000.

4. Transfer the value to a personal retirement bond (PRB).

5. Transfer the value to a new employer OPS.

6. Transfer the value to a public sector pension plan.

7. Transfer the value to a suitable overseas pension plan.

8. Access retirement benefits if age 50 or older, subject to specific conditions (see **Chapter 6**).

FIGURE 4.4: OPTIONS ON LEAVING AN EMPLOYMENT

Not entitled to employer contributions	Refund of own contributions if less than two years' qualifying service	Pension benefit in an employer OPS	If age 50+, take early retirement benefits

Leave the benefit in the existing OPS	Transfer to a PRSA if 15 years or less OPS service	Transfer to a PRB	Transfer to new employer OPS	Transfer to suitable overseas or public sector pension plan
Access benefits from age 50 onwards with trustee consent. Investment choice is limited to the options provided by the existing OPS	If transfer value is greater than €10,000, a certificate of benefit comparision/ reason why statement may be required	Access benefits from age 50 onwards, provides diversification and investment choice, including self-directed options	Cannot access benefits on early retirement unless leaving new employment. Invesment choice is limited to the options provided by the new employer OPS	

OPS Vested Rights for Employees

An OPS must have rules on vested rights for employees regarding their entitlement to the employer contributions when leaving that employment.

- **Full vested rights** If an employee has full vested rights in an existing OPS, the employee is entitled to retain the value of the employer contributions, in addition to the value of their own contributions, on leaving employment, irrespective of how long the employee has been a member of the OPS. If an employee has less than two years' qualifying service, the employee has the option to take a refund of the value of their own contributions. If the refund option is exercised by the employee, the employee is not entitled to the value of the employer contributions.
- **Nil vested rights** If an employee has nil vested rights in the existing OPS and has less than two years' qualifying service, the employee is not entitled to retain the value of the employer contributions, only the value of their own contributions.
- A refund of the value of an employee's own contributions is subject to tax at the standard rate, deducted at source by the pension plan provider. If a refund to an employee is made, the value of the employer contributions is refunded to the employer (this refund is treated as a trading receipt).

An employee benefit in an OPS becomes a 'preserved benefit' if an employee has at least two years' qualifying service.

If the employee had previously transferred in benefits from a previous employer OPS to the existing employer OPS, the service in the previous employer OPS is counted for the purposes of calculating qualifying service in the existing employer OPS. Therefore, if an employee leaves Employer A and goes to Employer B, their qualifying service in Employer A will count towards their length of qualifying service in the pension plan of Employer B.

Note: Prior to 1 June 2002, this minimum time-period for a benefit to become a 'preserved benefit' was five years of qualifying service, two years of which were completed after 1 January 1991, which may be relevant for employees who still have a retained benefit in a previous employer OPS that had been accumulated prior to 1 June 2002.

When a benefit is a 'preserved benefit', the employee retains the value of the employer contributions, in addition to the value of their own contributions, on leaving employment, and the employee is not entitled to take a refund of the value of their own contributions.

Accessing Benefits Before Normal Retirement Age on Early Retirement

Early retirement benefits can be taken from an OPS by employees aged 50 and upwards who have left employment. In defined benefit schemes, the rules may require employer and/or trustee consent for early retirement benefits to be paid. As discussed in **Chapter 3**, the OPS member can continue to work as an employee with another employer, or as a self-employed individual. Taking early retirement from an OPS does not preclude the individual from continuing to work elsewhere.

If an employee in an OPS directly or indirectly owns or controls more than 20% of the shares (with voting rights) in the employer company at any time in the three-year period prior to early retirement, the employee must sever all links with the company, including the disposal of their entire shareholding, in order to access benefits on early retirement.

Leaving Pension Benefits in Existing OPS

Many employees change employers and leave pension benefits in the pension plans provided by their previous employers. The employee is **not** obliged to move their benefits from the previous employer OPS, unless that OPS is winding up.

Leaving pension benefits in pension plans provided by previous employers can have the following benefits and consequences:

- The employee maintains the flexibility of access to retirement benefits from the previous employer pension plan from age 50 onwards (subject to trustee consent), without the employee having to retire from their current employment.
- Lack of advice and visibility on pension benefits in previous employer pension plans can arise over time. Employees normally do **not** receive ongoing advice from the advisor of the previous employer pension plan. The chosen investment allocation for the pension plan benefit

may not be reviewed/amended over time and may be inappropriate as investment markets change and/or as employee risk profiles change over time.

Transfer to a PRSA

Employees with up to 15 years' membership in the OPS as an active member (i.e. in employment with contributions being paid into the OPS) who are either leaving service or where the plan is being wound up can transfer the value in the OPS to a PRSA.

Standalone AVCs (i.e. AVCs that have been paid into a separate AVC plan that the employer has provided alongside the main OPS) can be transferred to a PRSA at any time and then become AVC PRSA contributions. *Note*: the 15-year rule does not apply to AVCs nor does the requirement for the employee to be leaving service or for the AVC plan to be winding up. Also, if the amount of the transfer is over €10,000, then a certificate of benefit comparison/reason why statement may be required (see below).

The chart in **Figure 4.5** below summarises the transfer rules/options for a transfer from an OPS to a PRSA.

FIGURE 4.5: TRANSFERRING FROM AN OPS TO A PRSA

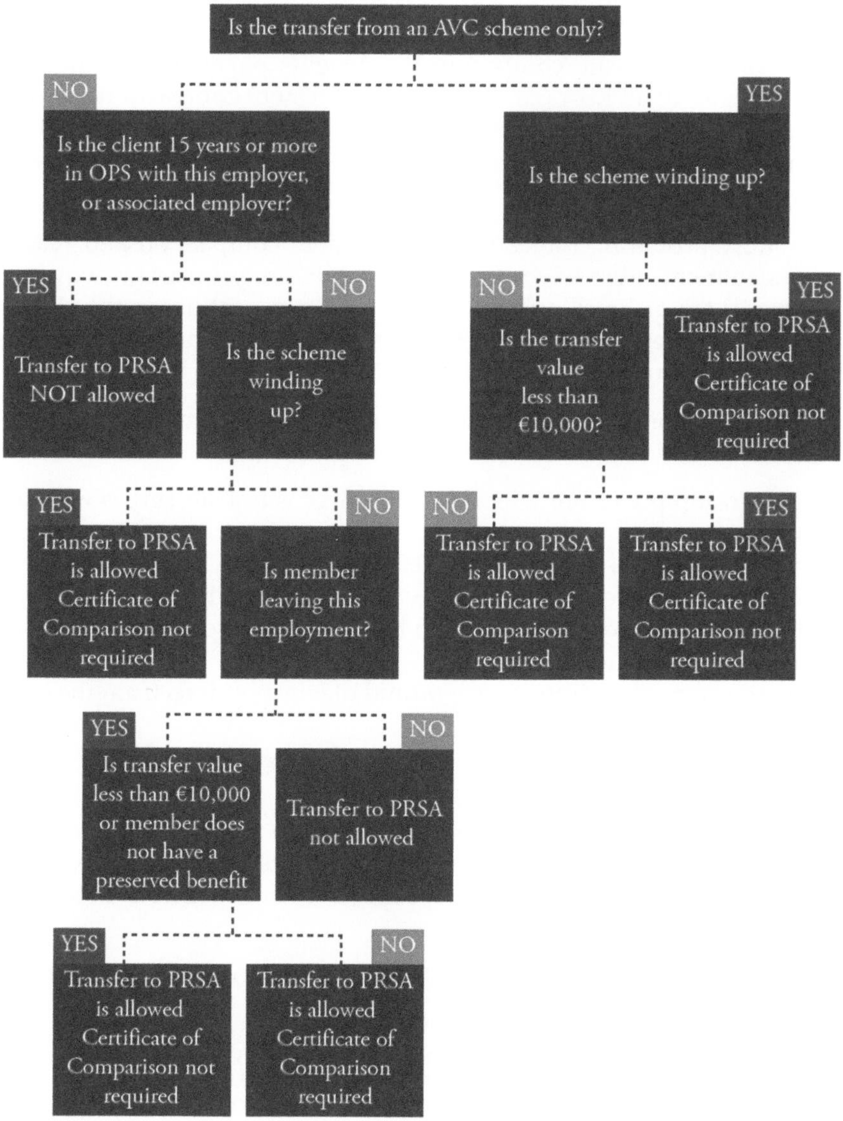

Is the transfer from an AVC scheme only?

NO

YES

Is the client 15 years or more in OPS with this employer, or associated employer?

Is the scheme winding up?

YES

Transfer to PRSA NOT allowed

NO

Is the scheme winding up?

NO

Is the transfer value less than €10,000?

YES

Transfer to PRSA is allowed Certificate of Comparison not required

YES

Transfer to PRSA is allowed Certificate of Comparison not required

NO

Is member leaving this employment?

NO

Transfer to PRSA is allowed Certificate of Comparison required

YES

Transfer to PRSA is allowed Certificate of Comparison not required

YES

Is transfer value less than €10,000 or member does not have a preserved benefit

NO

Transfer to PRSA not allowed

YES

Transfer to PRSA is allowed Certificate of Comparison not required

NO

Transfer to PRSA is allowed Certificate of Comparison required

Source: Irish Life, Pension Transfer Matrix & FAQ, p. 3 (with the permission of Irish Life)

In order to transfer benefits from an OPS into a PRSA (other than in a pension plan wind-up situation), the PRSA provider (or an intermediary acting on its behalf) must provide the customer with:

- a written certificate comparing the benefits payable from the OPS with those of a PRSA (i.e. a certificate of benefit comparison); and
- a statement of the reasons why it would be in the best interests of the individual to transfer assets from the plan to the PRSA (a 'reasons why statement').

The entity providing the certificate of benefit comparison and reason why statement must have professional indemnity insurance cover in place of at least €1 million per client. (In practice, entities in the market may not be prepared to provide these documents, thus reducing the ability of OPS members to transfer to PRSAs.)

Some exemptions from the requirement for a certificate of benefit comparison/reason why statement are as follows:

- the pension plan from which the employee is transferring is winding up;
- the transfer value is less than €10,000;
- the transfer value represents the value of accrued benefits (employer and employee) to a member who has less than two years' qualifying service with the employer;
- the transfer value represents a refund of contributions from the OPS.

Transfer to a Personal Retirement Bond (PRB)

A personal retirement bond (PRB), also known as a 'buy-out bond', is a pension plan structure purchased by the trustees of an OPS, with the same tax-exempt status as an approved OPS, and which is effected in an employee's own name.

A transfer of an employee's benefit from an OPS to a PRB can be made:

- when an employee has left employment; or
- when the OPS is being wound up by the employer.

In addition, in specific cases, pension benefits in overseas pension plans can be transferred to a PRB.

A PRB is a commonly used pension structure and can be an advantageous option for an employee for a number of reasons, including:

- The employee maintains the flexibility of access to retirement benefits from the previous employer pension plan from age 50 onwards (subject to the rules of the previous employer pension plan), without the employee having to retire from their current employment.

- A PRB can provide the employee with improved visibility and control over the investment of the funds in the pension plan. PRBs are offered by a number of pension plan providers with access to a wide range of investment options, including investments in alternative assets and strategies, and in direct assets such as listed shares and deposits, options that may not be available in either the previous or current employer pension plans. Accordingly, a PRB can provide greater diversification compared to a group OPS that may only provide a limited range of investment options. (See the section on "The Importance of Diversification" in **Chapter 2**.)
- The employee can receive ongoing advice in respect of the investments in the PRB from the advisor who advised the employee on the PRB option.

In some cases, the annual management charges on a PRB may be higher than the previous or current employer pension plans, as a PRB is an individual arrangement, unlike a group plan (which can benefit from lower charges due to economies of scale and/or the employer separately paying towards the plan costs).

Transfer to New Employer OPS

Another common option for employees is to transfer the benefit in a previous employer pension plan to the pension plan provided by their current employer. This option ensures that pension plan benefits are maintained in a single pension structure and extends the qualifying service in the existing OPS, because, as outlined above, after the transfer, the service in the previous employer plan is counted for the purposes of calculating qualifying service in the existing OPS.

However, as also discussed in **Chapters 3** and **6**, retirement benefits from pension plans from previous employments that have **not** been transferred into a current employer's pension plan can typically be accessed from age 50 onwards as required, which allows employees to avail of these benefits while still in employment.

EXAMPLE **4.1**: EMPLOYEE OPTIONS FOR PENSION PLAN FROM PREVIOUS EMPLOYMENT

Paul is aged 52 and is in employment. He has a retained benefit, valued at €80,000, in a previous employer pension plan. Paul has the option of accessing benefits from this pension plan **without** having to 'retire' from his current job. The options for accessing the benefits include taking a lump sum of 25% of the pension plan value, i.e. a lump sum of €20,000, and investing the balance of €60,000 in a retirement fund. Paul can also continue to pay into the pension plan in respect of his current employment.

Finally, it is worth noting that in some cases transferring a pension benefit in a previous employer pension plan to a pension plan provided by a current employer can limit the options for employees in some cases. The investment options available for the benefit will be limited to those provided by the current employer pension plan. Group plans provided by employers usually have a limited range of investment funds for employees to select for the investment of the pension contributions, whereas individual plans, such as the PRB structure discussed above, typically provide a wider range of investment options, which can include share trading and property investment options, as well as a wide choice of investment funds.

Transfer to an Overseas Pension Plan

The option to transfer a pension benefit to an overseas pension plan, which may be relevant for persons from overseas who work in Ireland for a specific period, or for Irish citizens who are moving abroad, will depend on:

- Confirmation that the overseas pension plan is a bona fide pension plan established for the purposes of providing retirement benefits (as defined by section 770 of the Taxes Consolidation Act 1997) that is approved by the appropriate regulatory authority in the relevant jurisdiction.
- If the transfer is to another EU Member State, the overseas pension plan must be operated or managed in accordance with specific EU rules. The pension plan administrator must be resident in an EU Member State.

- The willingness of the receiving pension plan to accept transfer in from an overseas pension plan. (Not all overseas pension plans have rules that permit transfers in from pension plans in other jurisdictions.)

In the event that an individual's pension plan benefit cannot be transferred overseas, the benefit can remain in an Irish pension plan and the normal rules for accessing retirement benefits from the plan in Ireland should still apply for the individual, irrespective of where they are actually residing overseas.

As discussed in **Chapter 1**, the EU has introduced a framework for the creation of a pan-European personal pension product (PEPP), which should facilitate the transfer of pension benefits between EU Member States.

Redundancy Payments and Pension Plans

At the time of writing, the statutory redundancy payment for employees consists of two weeks' pay for every year of service and one further week's pay, to a maximum earnings limit of €600 per week (€31,200 per year). Statutory redundancy payments are tax free.

If a redundancy payment is higher than the statutory amount, some or all of the amount above the statutory amount can also be tax free. This tax-free amount is the **higher** of the following three exemptions:

1. **Basic Exemption**: the basic tax-exempt amount is €10,160, plus €765 per complete year of service in employment.
2. **Increased Exemption:** the basic tax-exempt amount above may be increased by €10,000 if:

   - the employee has not claimed the increased exemption or SCSB (see below) in the previous 10 years;

   AND
   - the employee is not a member of an OPS relating to that employment, or the employee irrevocably gives up the right to receive a lump sum from such an OPS.

If an employee receives or is entitled to receive a pension lump sum, the increased exemption of €10,000 is reduced by the present-day value of the tax-free pension lump sum.

The pension lump sum is calculated in accordance with the rules for lump sums on early retirement (see **Chapter 6**). This amount is then rolled forward to normal retirement age (see the section on "Normal Retirement Age and Early Retirement" in **Chapter 6**) to allow for inflation and discounted back to calculate the present-day value.

If the present-day value of the tax-free lump sum from the pension plan is more than €10,000 and the employee is not giving up the right to the lump sum, the increased exemption does not apply.

3. **Standard Capital Superannuation Benefit (SCSB)**: the formula for calculating the SCSB is:

$$\frac{A \times B}{15} - C$$

A = average annual earnings over last three years of service ending on the date of termination. The earnings figure is gross salary before employee contributions to an approved pension plan, and can include benefits-in-kind, bonuses, etc.

B = number of complete years of service.

C = present-day value of any tax-free pension lump sum received or receivable from an occupational pension scheme relating to the employment.

If the employee irrevocably waives the right to receive a tax-free lump sum from the pension plan before the date of termination, then C will be €0, which would result in a higher tax-exempt amount in most cases.

The lump sum to be waived refers to any/all lump sums from approved OPSs relating to the employer paying the termination payment and does not include lump sums payable from a personal pension plan or a PRSA.

The remaining balance of the redundancy payment (after statutory redundancy and the additional tax-exempt amount), if any, is subject to income tax at the employee's marginal rate and USC, as appropriate. (PRSI does not apply.)

Note: a lifetime limit on tax-exempt redundancy payments applies. The lifetime limit is currently €200,000.

An example of the above calculation is contained in **Example 4.2** below.

EXAMPLE 4.2: CALCULATION OF TAX ON A REDUNDANCY PAYMENT

Alan is being made redundant at age 50 after 31 years of service. He is a member of his employer's OPS and the NRA is 60.

Alan's gross weekly pay is €800 and his average annual pay over the last three years was €41,600.

The present-day value of his lump sum entitlement from the OPS is calculated at €27,000.

The employer is paying four weeks' redundancy pay in total (i.e. statutory redundancy payment + an ex gratia payment) for each year of service, so Alan's redundancy payment is:

$$(4 \times 31) \times €800 = €99,200$$

The taxable portion of this payment is calculated as follows:

Tax-free statutory redundancy €600 × 63 (i.e. two weeks for each year of service + one further week) = €37,800

Balance of redundancy payment after statutory redundancy amount = €61,400 (i.e. €99,200 – €37,800)

The tax-exempt amount of the balance of the redundancy payment is the higher of following:

1. Basic exemption: €10,160, plus €765 per complete year of service = €33,875
2. Increased exemption: not applicable as the present-day OPS tax free lump sum > €10,000
3. SCSB: €41,600 × 31 years/15 years – €27,000 OPS tax free lump sum = €58,973

Therefore, the total tax-free amount = **€96,773** (€37,800 statutory redundancy + €58,973 SCSB).

Taxable portion of the redundancy payment = **€2,427** (€99,200 redundancy payment – €96,773 tax-free amount).

Note: under the SCSB option above, Alan is **not** waiving his right to receive a tax-free lump sum from the pension plan. If Alan waived this right, the SCSB amount would be higher and would result in the entire redundancy payment being tax free.

Life Insurance for Employees

In addition to providing a pension plan, many employers will also provide life insurance (such as life cover and disability cover) for employees as a group, as part of their employee benefits package. (**Chapter 5** covers life insurance taken out by/for an individual, i.e. not for a group of employees.)

Life insurance provided by employers for employees typically consists of:

- life cover (known as 'death-in-service cover'); and
- income protection/disability cover.

When provided by employers, these benefits are typically provided on a 'group' basis, i.e. for a group of individuals, rather than on an 'individual' basis, i.e. for a single individual. These group life insurance arrangements differ from individual life insurance in that individual underwriting may not be required for the individuals in the group, subject to the 'non-medical limits' for the group (see the "Non-medical Limit" section below), whereas individual underwriting (such as health questionnaires, medical reports, medical tests, financial questionnaires, etc.) is required when arranging individual life insurance.

In addition, the costs for group life insurance are typically reviewed periodically, whereas the costs for individual life insurance can be fixed for the term of the insurance or can increase at a defined rate. Accordingly, life insurance costs for employers can increase if the age profile of the workforce becomes older over time.

Death-in-service Cover

Death-in-service (DIS) cover provided for employees typically provides a lump sum payable in the event of the death of an employee. The cover level is usually a multiple of salary, for example, four times the salary of the deceased employee. DIS cover can also provide a pension income payable to dependants (for a higher insurance premium cost).

DIS cover is provided under a trust arrangement, whereby the employer or another nominated party acts as the trustee. (*Note*: formal trustee training is **not** required for the trustee of a DIS plan.) DIS cover can be provided alongside the pension plan within a single group occupational pension scheme structure, i.e. in one combined plan within a single trust. However, in the case of a group PRSA plan, a separate DIS cover plan is required if the employer wishes to provide DIS cover, i.e. DIS cover cannot be provided by the PRSA plan.

The death benefit is payable to the beneficiaries of a deceased employee or to a person (normally the spouse or other dependant of the deceased employee) chosen by the trustee. Employees can choose to complete a death benefit nomination form (also known as a 'Letter of Wishes'), in order to assist the trustees in determining the person(s) who should receive the payment of a DIS benefit in the event of the employee's death.

The trustee has a legal duty to ensure that the benefit is paid to the appropriate person(s). A nomination form can assist in this process by providing guidance to the trustees; however, a nomination form is not binding on the trustees (as an employee's personal circumstances may change and the employee may not always remember to update his or her nomination form to reflect the change in personal circumstances – therefore, a nomination form may not always be an accurate expression of the employee's wishes at the time of death).

Income Protection/Disability Cover

The State Illness Benefit is an income benefit payable by the State to individuals who are unable to work due to illness or injury. The income benefit is not means-tested and is approximately €10,000 per annum for a single person (at the time of writing), which is a very basic level of income for many working persons. Accordingly, income protection cover that insures income on an ongoing basis is a very important type of insurance cover.

Typically, income protection/disability cover benefits can be payable to employees after a deferred period (the deferred period is usually 13 weeks or 26 weeks) after the individual becomes unable to work due to illness or injury. Income protection cover does not provide a benefit during shorter periods of being out of work.

Premium protection cover is also available to provide for ongoing pension contributions to be paid to the employee's pension plan, in addition to salary payments to the employee who is unable to work. In addition, the DIS costs for the employee would continue to be covered, so that the employee would continue to be covered for DIS cover while unable to work.

The amount of the income benefit payment to an employee who is unable to work can increase each year (to allow for inflation) or can remain fixed. The income protection insurance premium cost is higher if this increasing benefit feature is included (known as an 'escalation feature').

Non-medical Limit

A non-medical limit is the maximum sum assured that an insurer will underwrite on an individual without seeking medical evidence. On this basis, employees (who are covered) will be automatically insured up to an agreed limit without having to complete health questionnaires or undergo a medical examination. **Example 4.3** below contains an example of a non-medical limit for DIS cover.

EXAMPLE 4.3: NON-MEDICAL LIMIT FOR DIS COVER

A non-medical limit of €600,000 has been set by the insurance provider for ABC Limited for DIS cover of four times salary for employees. On this basis, all employees with salaries under or at €150,000 will automatically be covered for DIS cover of four times their salaries.

The CEO of ABC Limited has a salary of €200,000; therefore, DIS cover up to €800,000 (four times salary) can be provided for the CEO. The CEO is **automatically** covered up to the non-medical limit of €600,000; the CEO will be required to undergo medical underwriting (involving, for example, completing a health questionnaire and/or attending a consultation with a medical practitioner) in order to determine if the DIS cover can be increased from €600,000 to €800,000 for the CEO.

Non-medical limit amounts will vary depending on plan size and the level of benefits. The minimum member number for non-medical limits is typically five (although some insurance providers may have a lower minimum). If an employer has fewer than five employees to be covered, a non-medical limit would not be provided and all employees would be required to undergo individual medical underwriting, irrespective of salary levels.

Non-medical limits are calculated based on the average cover per employee covered. For example, the insurer New Ireland Assurance calculates non-medical limits as follows:

- **DIS limit**: twice average employee plan benefits plus 10% of total value of death benefits. If a dependant's pension is also covered, the value of death benefits includes the capitalised value of the pension that is payable to dependants or children on death. (*Note:* 'capitalised value' is an actuarial calculation of a single lump sum to cover a future stream of dependants' pension payments.)
- **Income protection limit**: the average income protection benefit for all employees plus 5% of the total value of income protection benefits. If pension and DIS premiums are also covered, the value of the income protection benefit includes the pension contributions and the DIS cost.

Continuation Option

DIS and income protection cover plans can include a continuation option that is available at an additional insurance premium cost. A continuation option provides a member leaving employment with the option to continue with DIS/income protection cover by taking a policy in their own name at their own cost, without being required to provide evidence of health, subject to terms and conditions.

Costs

Annual costs for employers for DIS cover can be in the range of 0.25% to 1% of annual salary. Annual costs for employers for income protection cover can be in the range of 0.5% to 2.5% of annual salary. Premiums can be paid by the employer annually in advance or on a periodic basis during the year (monthly/quarterly, etc.).

Note: actual premiums will depend on a variety of factors, including the occupations and age profiles of employees, applicable rates, claims history, etc., and may differ significantly from the guideline costs above.

Examples of Employee Pension Plan and Life Insurance Benefits in Practice

Figure 4.6 below contains a summary of the employee pension plan and life insurance benefits provided by actual employers (research by Simon Shirley Advisors Limited in 2019).

EXAMPLE 4.4: EMPLOYEE PENSION PLAN AND LIFE INSURANCE BENEFITS IN PRACTICE

Sector	Country of Origin	No. Employees	Employer Pension Contribution	Vesting Period	Pension Plan Eligibility	Life Cover	Long-term Disability	Disability Deferred Period
Aircraft Leasing	UK	< 10	10%	2 years	Month 7 (day 1 snr. managers)	4 × salary	75% salary less SIB	13 weeks
Biotech	Ireland	10+	5%	2 years	Day 1	None	None	N/A
Energy	UK	<10	3%	Day 1	Month 7	4 × salary	None	N/A
Financial Services	Ireland	< 10	5%	2 years	Day 1	4 × salary	75% salary less SIB	13 weeks
Financial Services	Ireland	50+	5%	Day 1	Day 1	4 × salary	None	N/A
Financial Services	Ireland	30+	10%	Day 1	Day 1	4 × salary	75% salary less SIB	13 weeks
Financial Services	USA	100+	3%	Day 1	Day 1	4 × salary	75% salary less SIB	26 weeks
Financial Services	Canada	50+	10%	2 years	1 Year	4 × salary	75% salary less SIB	26 weeks
IT	USA	500+	4%	Day 1	Day 1	4 × salary	75% salary less SIB	13 weeks
IT	USA	30+	None	N/A	N/A	3 × salary	75% salary less SIB	26 weeks
IT	Ireland	40+	5%	1 year 50%	Day 1	4 × salary	67% salary less SIB	26 weeks
IT	UK	30+	3%	Day 1	Day 1	4 × salary	None	N/A
IT	USA	250+	6%	2 years	Month 7	4 × salary	75% salary less SIB	26 weeks

Sector	Country of Origin	No. Employees	Employer Pension Contribution	Vesting Period	Pension Plan Eligibility	Life Cover	Long-term Disability	Disability Deferred Period
IT	USA	80+	5%	1 year	Day 1	4 × salary	75% salary less SIB	13 weeks
IT	Ireland	80+	None	N/A	N/A	6 × salary	None	N/A
IT	USA	50+	None	N/A	N/A	4 × salary	75% salary less SIB	13 weeks
IT	USA	50+	4%	2 years	Month 7	4 × salary	75% salary less SIB	13 weeks
IT	USA	< 10	5%	2 years	Day 1	4 × salary	75% salary less SIB	13 weeks
IT	USA	< 10	5%	2 years	Day 1	4 × salary	75% salary less SIB	13 weeks
IT	USA	90+	50% match up to €4,000	2 years	Day 1	2 × salary	67% salary less SIB	13 weeks
IT	USA	20+	4%	2 years	Month 4	3 × salary	60% salary less SIB	13 weeks
IT	France	10+	4%	2 years	Month 4	4 × salary	75% salary less SIB	26 weeks
IT	USA	30+	4%	2 years	Day 1	4 × salary	75% salary less SIB	26 weeks
IT	Israel	20+	4%	2 years	Month 4	4 × salary	None	N/A
IT	Israel	30+	4%	Day 1	Day 1	4 × salary	75% salary less SIB	13 weeks
IT	USA	20+	None	N/A	N/A	4 × salary	75% salary less SIB	13 weeks
Leisure	USA	20+	3%	2 years	Year end	None	None	N/A
Medical Supplies	Ireland	70+	7% (mgt. only)	2 years	Day 1	4 × salary	75% salary less SIB	26 weeks
Telecoms	Ireland	100+	Flexible benefits option	Day 1	Day 1	4 × salary	None	N/A
SIB = State Illness Benefit								

103

10 Key Points: Employee Pension and Life Insurance Plans

1. Attractive employee benefit packages, including an employer-sponsored pension plan, have become increasingly important for hiring and retaining staff.

2. For many employees, pension plan benefits built up during employment will be their most important financial asset in retirement.

3. Pension plans provided by employers for employees are structured as an occupational pension scheme (OPS), and/or a personal retirement savings account (PRSA). These plans are typically provided on a group basis, i.e. for more than one employee.

4. Employers are legally obliged to provide employees with access to a pension plan. The minimum requirement is the provision of access to a standard PRSA.

5. Employees in an OPS have the option to make additional voluntary contributions (AVCs) subject to age-related percentage limits, and may have the option of backdating the tax relief on AVCs to the previous year.

6. Employees have a number of options on leaving an employment regarding their benefits in an OPS/PRSA.

7. Retirement benefits from pension plans from previous employments that have not been transferred into a current employer's pension plan can typically be accessed from age 50 onwards, as required, which allows employees to avail of these benefits while still in employment.

8. Life cover/disability cover provided by employers for employees typically consists of death-in-service cover and income protection/disability cover, which is provided on a 'group' basis, i.e. for a group of individuals, rather than on an 'individual' basis, i.e. for a single individual.

9. Group death-in-service cover and income protection/disability cover will typically have a non-medical limit. This limit is the maximum sum assured that an insurer will underwrite on an individual without seeking medical evidence. On this basis, employees (who are covered) will be automatically insured up to an agreed limit without having to complete health questionnaires or undergo a medical examination.

10. Indicative annual premiums for death-in-service cover can be in the range of 0.25% to 1% of annual salary. Indicative annual premiums for income protection cover can be in the range of 0.5% to 2.5% of annual salary.

5.

Life Insurance for Individuals and Businesses

- Introduction
- Types of Life Insurance
- Life Cover
- Income Protection/Disability Cover
- Specified Illness Cover
- Costs of Insurance
- Tax Relief Available
- Life Insurance for Businesses

Introduction

Insurance is an important component of business and personal financial planning (which includes pension planning). Many of us have several types of insurance, such as insurance for property, car, health, travel, etc. Many of these types of insurance are essential; however, by far the biggest financial risk for you and your dependants is the risk of your death and/or the risk of you becoming ill and unable to work. Despite the importance of insuring against these risks, many individuals do not fully appreciate the appropriate levels of insurance required for adequate financial protection for themselves and for their families, and/or may not be aware of the different structures and tax reliefs available.

Whereas **Chapter 4** has covered life insurance provided by employers for employees as a group, this chapter covers life insurance arranged on an individual basis (i.e. life insurance taken out by individuals and by businesses to cover individuals rather than to cover employees as a group).

In this chapter we will examine:

- types of life insurance;
- life cover;
- income protection/disability cover;
- specified illness cover;
- costs of insurance;
- tax relief available;
- life insurance for businesses.

(*Note*: in this book, the generic term 'life insurance' refers to the typical insurances provided by life insurance companies, such as life cover, income protection/disability cover and specified illness cover.)

Types of Life Insurance

There are three main types of life insurance:

1. **Life cover** provides a lump sum payment in the event of death. The cost of specific types of life cover may qualify for personal income tax relief or business tax relief.
2. **Income protection/disability cover** provides an **ongoing** income in the event of becoming unable to work due to illness or injury.

The cost of income protection cover typically qualifies for personal income tax relief or business tax relief.

3. **Specified illness cover:** provides a **single** lump sum payment in the event of the diagnosis of a specified illness (such as cancer, heart attack, stroke, etc.). The cost of this cover is generally not allowable for tax relief.

The importance and appropriate levels of these types of cover depend on individual personal circumstances. In an ideal world, we would all have the maximum levels of all types of insurance; however, the reality for many of us is that insurance is often a balancing act between weighing up the ongoing cost against the seriousness of the risk.

As a general rule of thumb:

- If you are working and do **not** have dependants (such as children), you should have income protection cover for most of your income. Your ability to earn an ongoing income is likely to be your most important financial asset.
- If you have dependants (such as children), you should have adequate life cover for your family's benefit in the event of your death (in addition to life cover on your home mortgage) and you should also have adequate income protection cover, as described above.
- Though specified illness cover can be important, in general, you should only consider specified illness cover **after** you have ensured that you have adequate levels of life cover and income protection cover. Specified illness cover generally costs more than life cover.
- Business owners in partnership (partners or shareholders) should have life cover (and should consider specified illness cover), in order to:
  - provide funds to purchase the shareholding of a deceased partner/shareholder (or a partner/shareholder who is seriously ill); and
  - provide funds to compensate the business for loss of profits or to repay business loans in the event of death or serious illness of partner/shareholder.

As discussed in the "Life Insurance for Employees" section in **Chapter 4**, if relevant, your employer may provide life cover and income protection/disability cover.

These three types of life insurance, i.e. life cover, income protection/disability cover, and specified illness cover are discussed in more detail in the following sections.

Life Cover

Life cover provides a lump sum payment in the event of death. The most common reasons for taking out life cover are as follows:

- **family protection**: providing a lump sum for the financial security for dependants (such as spouse, partner or children);
- **mortgage protection**: providing a lump sum to pay off a mortgage;
- **business protection**: providing a lump sum to compensate a business for loss of profits or to repay business loans arising from the death of a key person or to purchase the shareholding of a deceased shareholder.

Life cover is typically arranged as either:

- **Term cover**: this is the most common type of life cover. Term cover has a specific term, for example '20 years', 'to age 65', etc. The premiums (i.e. the cost) for this cover are typically fixed at the outset, irrespective of changes to personal circumstances that may occur in future, such as changes in health, therefore the cost remains the same throughout the term of the policy, irrespective of any change to personal circumstances (unless an indexation option is selected at the outset – see below); or
- **Whole-of-life cover**: this type of life cover does not have a specific term but provides cover for death at any stage, provided the premiums have been paid up to date. The premiums for this life cover can be reviewable and can increase as a person becomes older. Some of the premiums may be used to build up a savings element in the policy. Whole-of-life cover is typically used for inheritance tax planning purposes.

A life cover policy (i.e. providing either term cover or whole of life cover) can include a number of options or product features that are selected when arranging the policy, such as:

- **Single life, joint life or dual life** Single life covers one person only. Joint life is typically used for mortgage protection cover for a mortgage in joint names; for example, life cover for a mortgage in the names of two spouses whereby one payment occurs in the event of the death of one or both persons covered. Dual life cover provides two payments in the event of the death of the two persons covered and can be used to cover both spouses for family protection for dependants.
- **Indexation** If this option is selected, both the amount of life cover and the cost will increase each year. This option is used to protect the real value of the life cover against the effects of inflation over time.

111

- **Medical-free conversion** Consists of an option to extend the cover beyond the end of the specific term without having to provide additional medical evidence (subject to specific conditions).

The cost of life cover for self-employed individuals and individuals in 'non-pensionable' employment can be structured so that the cost is allowable for income tax relief in the same manner as personal pension contributions, i.e. the cost may qualify for income tax relief (within age-related limits). This insurance cover is often referred to as 'pension term cover'. (See the section on "Personal Pension Plans" in **Chapter 3**.)

The cost of employer-paid life cover for employees is allowable as a trading expense for business tax purposes – see the "Life Insurance for Employees" section in **Chapter 4**.

Calculating the Level of Life Cover Required

The level of life cover you require depends on your personal circumstances. If you have young children, then life cover (to provide a lump sum payable on death) of 10 to 15 times your gross annual earnings should be considered. At first glance, this level of life cover may appear excessive. However, **Example 5.1** below highlights the extent of the level of life cover that may be required:

EXAMPLE 5.1: CALCULATING THE LEVEL OF LIFE COVER REQUIRED

Jane has annual gross earnings of €60,000, with after-tax earnings of €3,000 per month, i.e. €36,000 per annum. She has young children. Assume that Jane's children will be financially dependent on her for the next 20 years.

Over the next 20 years, assuming that Jane's earnings grow by 3% per annum, and ignoring additional earnings increases arising from career progression, Jane will earn a total of approximately €967,000 after tax. In the event of the Jane's death, her family would have lost these future earnings and thus require a lump sum that is sufficient to provide these future earnings over the next 20 years (and possibly longer).

Life cover to provide a lump sum in excess of €700,000 (i.e. 12 times Jane's annual gross earnings) would be required in order to provide this income, assuming an average annual after-tax rate of investment return of 3% on the investment of the lump sum, and assuming that the lump sum has been fully withdrawn for income needs over time by the end of 20 years, i.e. the lump sum of €700,000 has been entirely spent by the end of the twentieth year.

For stay-at-home parents who take care of children, life cover of at least €300,000 should be considered, in order to provide for the cost of a full-time childminder for, say, 15 years.

The need for life cover typically diminishes as retirement approaches, as children may no longer be financially dependent and mortgages and other financial commitments may have reduced or ceased. Thankfully, the cost of life cover that ceases at age 65 is relatively inexpensive for healthy, non-smoking individuals in their 30s and 40s (see the indicative cost of life cover in **Figure 5.1** below).

'Whole-of-life' cover is life cover that can continue throughout your life until you die. This type of life cover is more expensive than life cover that ends on a specified date (such as age 65) and can be used in order to pay for inheritance tax that may arise on death in accordance with Revenue rules, or to provide for other costs that may arise on death.

As discussed in **Chapter 4**, if an individual is in employment, their employer may provide a level of life insurance benefits, such as life cover based on a multiple of their salary (e.g. four times salary) known as death-in-service (DIS) cover; and some employers also provide income protection/disability cover. Depending on their circumstances, employees may need to supplement this cover by personally arranging additional insurance.

EXAMPLE 5.2: 'TOPPING UP' DEATH-IN-SERVICE COVER

Patricia and Martin are both working and have three young children. Patricia's salary is €80,000 and Martin's salary is €60,000. Both are covered for DIS cover of four times salary by their respective employers, i.e. Patricia has DIS cover of €320,000 and Martin has DIS cover of €240,000.

Patricia and Martin wish to provide additional financial protection for their family in the event of either or both of their deaths, and decide to arrange personal life cover of €500,000 on Patricia's life and €500,000 on Martin's life. This cover can be provided under one life insurance policy, on a dual-life basis, with a single premium payable monthly or annually.

Income Protection/Disability Cover

Income protection cover provides an ongoing monthly income in the event of an individual becoming unable to work due to illness or injury. This type of insurance cover is also known as 'disability cover' or 'permanent health insurance'.

As the State Illness Benefit provides only a very basic level of income, income protection cover that insures income on an ongoing basis is a very important type of insurance.

The cost of Revenue-approved personal income protection cover that is arranged by an individual is allowable for personal income tax relief at the individual's higher rate of income tax (currently up to 40%) subject to limits.

An example of a formal definition of 'disability' for an income protection policy (with the permission of insurance provider Aviva) is set out in **Example 5.3** below.

EXAMPLE 5.3: POLICY DEFINITION OF 'DISABILITY'

"A period throughout which, in the opinion of Aviva, the life insured because of illness or injury due to an identifiable and recognised medical cause, is totally unable to carry out their Essential Duties and is not engaged in any other gainful employment or self-employment. Essential Duties means those duties, which cannot, in the opinion of Aviva, be omitted without preventing the life insured from carrying out their Normal Occupation. Normal Occupation means the life insured's normal principal occupation or occupations during the twelve months ending on the day immediately prior to disability."

The main features of income protection cover arranged by individuals are as follows:

- Occupations are divided into four 'occupation classes' ranging from Occupation Class 1 up to Occupation Class 4. Occupation Class 1 covers many non-manual office-based or clerical occupations and Occupation Class 4 covers some manual occupations. The cost of cover for Occupation Class 1 is lower than the cost for the other occupation classes, and the cost of cover is higher for higher occupation class numbers, i.e. the cost of cover for Occupation Class 3 is higher than the cost of cover for Occupation Class 2, and the cost of cover for Occupation Class 4 is higher than the cost of cover for Occupation Class 3. For example, an accountant would typically be classed under Occupation Class 1 and a motor mechanic would typically be classed under Occupation Class 4. Cover is generally not available for some occupations, for example farmers and taxi drivers.
- Cover of up to 75% of earnings is available, less the single person State Illness Benefit (approximately €10,000 per annum at the time of writing).
- The ceasing age (i.e. age up to which the risk is covered on the life assured insured by the insurance policy) for the cover can be up to age 70. The cost of cover with an older ceasing age is higher than the cost of cover with a younger ceasing age.

- The benefit is typically payable on a monthly basis after a deferred period following the date of becoming unable to work. Deferred periods from four weeks up to 52 weeks are available. The cost of cover with shorter deferred periods is higher than the cost of cover with longer deferred periods.
- Cover is available on a **guaranteed basis**, whereby the level of cover and cost is fixed from commencement, and on a **reviewable basis**, whereby the level of cover and cost is reviewable on a periodic basis during the term of the cover. At commencement, the cost of cover on a guaranteed basis is higher than the cost of cover on a reviewable basis.
- Indexation of cover is available, whereby the level of cover and cost can be indexed each year at an agreed rate. Escalation of benefit is also available, whereby in the event of a claim, the benefit payable would escalate by an agreed amount each year.

Specified Illness Cover

Specified illness cover provides a single lump-sum payment in the event of the diagnosis of a specified illness. The cover is usually available on a stand-alone basis or in conjunction with life cover. The cost of this cover is generally not allowable for tax relief.

A wide range of illnesses are covered and a reduced level of cover can apply to some illnesses. Examples of the illnesses, conditions and events covered include cancer, heart attack and stroke. For further examples, see www.aviva.ie/content/dam/aviva-public/ie/pdfs/specified-illness-definitions-guide.pdf.

Costs of Insurance

Figures 5.1 to **5.3** below list the indicative costs of cover, based on standard non-smoker rates (as at time of writing). The costs are based on the lowest quoted rates that the author has obtained from the main life insurance providers in Ireland (before any applicable discounts).

Note: a significant number of options are available, which can reduce or increase the cost of cover. The term of the cover can have a significant impact on cost, particularly in the case of income protection cover, whereby the cost can be reduced by 20–30% by reducing the term from age 65 to age 60.

The life cover and specified illness cover costs shown are for fixed cover for a single person, whereby the level of cover and the cost is fixed and does not change during the term of the cover. Indexing cover is also available, whereby the level of cover and cost increases each year (to protect against inflation).

FIGURE 5.1: INDICATIVE COST OF LIFE COVER OF €500,000

Age Now	Term of Cover	Monthly Cost*
30	To age 65	€40
40	To age 65	€56
50	To age 65	€100
60	To age 65	€147

* Monthly cost is before income tax relief, if applicable.

Figure 5.2 lists the indicative cost of indexing personal income protection cover of €50,000 per annum with guaranteed costs and a deferred period of 26 weeks for a Class 1 occupation.

FIGURE 5.2: INDICATIVE COST OF INDEXING INCOME PROTECTION COVER OF €50,000 PER ANNUM

Age Now	Term of Cover	Gross Monthly Cost	Net Monthly Cost*
30	To age 65	€77	€46
40	To age 65	€121	€73
50	To age 65	€214	€128
59	To age 65	€306	€184

* Net monthly cost is gross monthly cost less tax relief at 40%.

FIGURE 5.3: INDICATIVE COST OF SPECIFIED ILLNESS COVER OF €100,000

Age Now	Term of Cover	Monthly Cost
30	To age 65	€44
40	To age 65	€66
50	To age 65	€109
60	To age 65	€170

Tax Relief Available

The cost of life cover for self-employed individuals and individuals in 'non-pensionable' employment can be structured so that the cost is allowable for income tax relief in the same manner as personal pension contributions, i.e. the cost can qualify for income tax relief up to the higher rate of 40%. See the section on "Personal Pension Plans" in **Chapter 3**. (*Note*: this type of life cover, known as 'pension term cover', can only be arranged on a single life basis and the life cover **cannot** be assigned to a lender for mortgage purposes.)

If an individual's employer does not provide an OPS, then they are deemed to be in 'non-pensionable' employment. Also, if their employer provides access to a PRSA, they are deemed to be in non-pensionable employment, even if their employer makes contributions to the PRSA for their benefit. If their employer provides a death-in-service life cover scheme (subject to limits) but does not provide an OPS, the individual is still deemed to be in non-pensionable employment.

Figure 5.4 below contains a guide to the availability of tax relief on life cover for employees (tax relief is available for self-employed persons).

FIGURE 5.4: FOR EMPLOYEES: IS TAX RELIEF AVAILABLE ON YOUR LIFE COVER?

Does your employer provide a pension plan?

YES

NO

Is the pension plan an occupational pension scheme (OPS) or a PRSA?

OPS

PRSA

NO

YES

Personal tax relief is NOT available on your life cover costs

Personal tax relief is available on your life cover costs

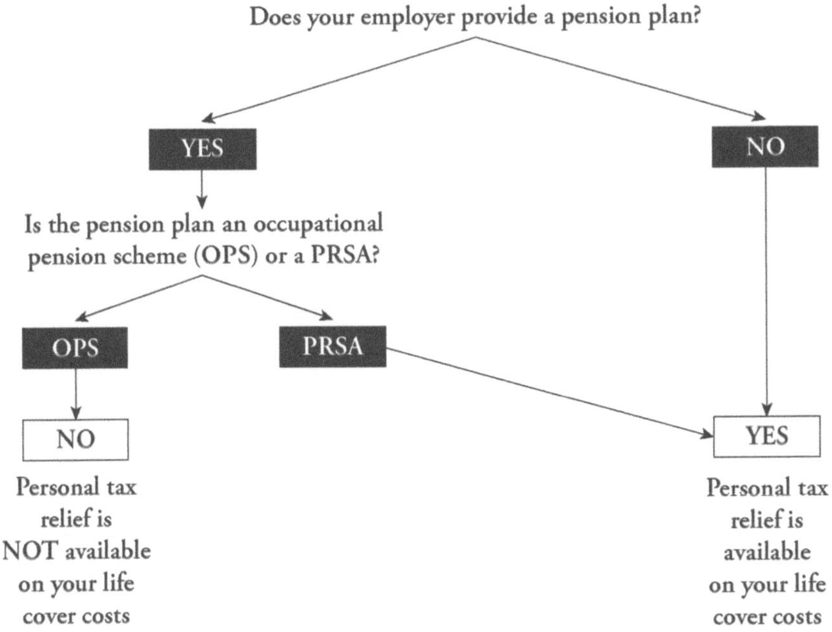

The cost to employers of providing death-in-service life cover and income protection cover for employees is allowable as a tax-deductible trading expense for business tax purposes and is not subject to Employer PRSI (similar to employer pension contributions – see the section on "Life Insurance for Employees" in **Chapter 4**).

Similarly, business owners who operate their business through a company and who are employed by the company can arrange death-in-service cover and income protection cover through the company, with the cost allowable as a tax-deductible trading expense for corporation tax purposes.

As previously mentioned, the cost of income protection cover, if paid by an individual, is allowable for personal income tax relief purposes at the higher rate (subject to limits).

Life Insurance for Businesses

The death of a shareholder/partner or a key employee can have significant adverse implications for a business and in some cases can threaten its continued existence. Life insurance can be structured and arranged to provide funds to purchase a deceased shareholder's/partner's share of a business from their estate, or to compensate a business for loss of profits or cover business loans in the event of the death of a key employee.

The odds/probability of one partner dying or becoming seriously ill before retirement in a two-person or three-person business are reflected in the statistics in **Figure 5.5** below.

FIGURE 5.5: PROBABILITY OF A PARTNER DYING OR BECOMING SERIOUSLY ILL BEFORE AGE 65

Age	Odds of one dying before 65 One man	Two men	Three men	Age	Odds of one dying or becoming seriously ill before 65 One man	Two men	Three men
40	12%	22%	32%	40	24%	42%	55%
45	11%	21%	30%	45	22%	39%	53%
50	10%	19%	30%	50	20%	36%	48%
55	8%	16%	28%	55	16%	30%	41%

(Source: CSO life tables (Ireland) 2010–2012)

(Source: CSO life tables (Ireland) 2010–2012) Critical illness tables (IC94) first published by the Society of Actuaries Ireland, 1994

Source: Irish Life, *Business Protection – Is It Something You Need to Consider?* (with the permission of Irish Life)

Life insurance for businesses consists of:

- **Shareholder cover:** to provide funds to purchase the share of a business from the estate of a deceased shareholder/partner – this cover is arranged as 'personal' shareholder cover or as 'corporate' shareholder cover, under a double-option buyback agreement (as discussed below).
- **Key person cover:** to compensate a business for loss of profits or to cover business loans in the event of the death of a key employee.

Shareholder Cover

Most shareholder and partnership agreements include provisions regarding the death of a shareholder/partner. Life cover can be taken out on the lives of each shareholder/partner, in conjunction with a 'double-option buyback agreement' to enable the surviving shareholders/partners to compel the estate of the deceased shareholder to sell the shares and to enable the estate to compel the surviving shareholders/partners to buy back the shares from the estate.

This life cover can be structured in several ways, whereby the cost of the life cover can be paid by the individual shareholders/partners (i.e. 'personal' shareholder cover) or can be paid by the business (i.e. 'corporate' shareholder cover). *Note*: the cost is **not** allowable for corporation tax or income tax relief, though the proceeds may be exempt from tax, depending on the structure and provided specific conditions are met.

Personal Shareholder Cover

Personal shareholder cover is structured so that the shareholders (or partners) enter into a personal legal agreement with each other to buy out a deceased shareholder's shares in the event of his or her death.

Personal life cover is arranged on the life of each shareholder, which is payable to the surviving shareholders on his or her death in order to provide the funds to fulfil their personal obligation under the legal agreement. The surviving shareholders can then use the proceeds of the life cover to buy out whoever inherits the shares of the deceased shareholder in line with the legal agreement. The personal life cover is arranged either on a 'life-of-another' basis or on an 'own-life-in-trust' basis.

The key features of a 'life-of-another' arrangement are as follows:

- each shareholder (or partner) covered by the legal agreement effects a life cover policy on the life of the other shareholders or partners;
- the cover on the policy should be equal to the estimated current value of the other shareholder's shareholding in the business (or share of the partnership);
- the proposing shareholder is the policy owner and pays the premiums from after-tax income;
- under current legislation, the proceeds of the policy should not be subject to tax in the hands of the policy owner, provided the policy owner has paid the premiums;
- this arrangement is straightforward if the business has two or three shareholders/partners; however, if there are more than three shareholders/partners, it can be cumbersome, as many life cover policies would be required (each shareholder has to effect an individual policy on each of the other shareholders, which multiplies the individual life cover policies required). In addition, this arrangement can be inflexible if a shareholder is exiting.

The key features of an 'own-life-in-trust' arrangement are as follows:

- each shareholder (or partner) covered by the legal agreement effects a life cover policy on their own life;
- the cover on the policy should be equal to the estimated current value of the shareholder's shareholding in the business (or share of the partnership);
- the shareholder pays the premiums on the policy;
- each policy is written under trust for the benefit of the other shareholders/partners;
- this arrangement is flexible in that the beneficiaries of the policy can be changed if the shareholder leaves the business or if the business protection agreement ceases;
- the policy proceeds should be exempt from tax in the hands of the surviving shareholders/partners, provided specific Revenue conditions are met.

EXAMPLE 5.4: PERSONAL SHAREHOLDER COVER ON AN 'OWN-LIFE-IN-TRUST' BASIS

Mary, John and Deirdre are shareholders in a company, valued at €1 million, with a double-option buyback agreement and life cover policies, as follows:

- Mary is a 40% shareholder. A life cover policy is taken out by Mary in trust for life cover of €400,000 on Mary's life. Mary pays the premiums.
- John is a 40% shareholder. A life cover policy is taken out by John in trust for life cover of €400,000 on John's life. John pays the premiums
- Deirdre is a 20% shareholder. A life cover policy is taken out by Deirdre in trust for life cover of €200,000 on Deirdre's life. Deirdre pays the premiums.

John dies. The life cover of €400,000 on John's life is paid out as follows:

- €266,667 to Mary, to enable Mary to purchase the shares from John's estate; and
- €133,333 to Deirdre, to enable Deirdre to purchase the shares from John's estate.

This 'personal' arrangement can be straightforward to arrange and the related legal and taxation issues are often also straightforward. However, the costs of the life cover are borne personally by the individual shareholders out of 'after-tax' personal income. If the company funds a 'personal' arrangement, the cost is treated by Revenue as a benefit-in-kind for each shareholder.

Corporate Shareholder Cover

Corporate shareholder cover is structured so that the company enters into a legal agreement with each of the shareholders to buy back shares from their estate in the event of their death.

The company takes out a life cover policy on each shareholder to provide funds to enable the company to fulfil its obligation under the legal agreement.

In the event of the death of a shareholder, the proceeds of the life cover policy are payable to the company to be used to buy back shares from the deceased's estate in line with the legal agreement.

This 'corporate' arrangement can be advantageous as the cost is incurred by the company (not by the individual shareholders), with no benefit-in-kind implications for the individual shareholders, because the policy proceeds are for the benefit of the company,

However, this option can be complex to set up because specific company law provisions need to be satisfied to enable a company to buy back its own shares. In addition, a number of conditions need to be satisfied to ensure the buyback of shares from the family of a deceased shareholder can be achieved in a tax-efficient manner, thus making this option unsuitable in specific circumstances. The preferred tax treatment is capital gains tax, which can apply if specific conditions are met.

Choosing whether the life cover suitable for a business is structured 'personal' shareholder/partner cover or 'corporate' shareholder/partner cover depends on a number of factors, some of which are listed in **Figure 5.6** below.

FIGURE 5.6: PERSONAL SHAREHOLDER COVER VS CORPORATE SHAREHOLDER COVER

	Personal shareholder cover	Corporate shareholder cover
Premiums paid by	The shareholder, personally	The company
Plan owned/ proceeds payable to	The shareholder personally/ the trustee of the life assurance plan	The company
Who will benefit?	Only shareholders who participate can benefit	All shareholders
Suitable for 'young' start-up companies?	Yes	No. The shares must be owned by the vendor for at least three years for the sale to be tax efficient.*
Suitable for invest-ment companies?	Yes	No. The company must be an unquoted trading company, i.e. a business that carries on a trade.*
Suitable where there are non-resident shareholders?	Yes	No. The vendor of the shares must be resident and ordinarily resident in the State for the sale to be tax efficient.*
Suitable if all shareholders not participating?	Only shareholders who participate can benefit	[Yes.] The company can effect cover on just one of its share-holders.

(* Specific tax advice is required regarding the tax treatment of the share purchase.)

Source: Irish Life, *Shareholder Protection: An Adviser's Guide* (with permission from Irish Life)

Specified illness cover can also be included (at a higher cost). On a separate but related note, all business partners should have income protection cover.

Key Person Insurance

Key person insurance provides a lump sum payment to the business in the event of the death (or serious illness) of a key employee, who may also be a shareholder and/or director. Key person insurance is taken out by a business, i.e. the business owns the policy.

The rationale for key person insurance is to provide financial compensation to a business in respect of the costs/losses that may arise in the event of the death or illness of a key employee. For many businesses, the 'human' assets are the most important and valuable assets of the business.

The amount or level of life and/or illness cover to be arranged for a key person should be based on the estimated costs/losses that may arise in the event of their death or serious illness.

In practice, accurately estimating the costs/losses can be difficult unless the key person insurance is structured to cover a loan taken out by the business, as the cover should equal the amount of the loan. In general, acceptable estimates can be based on one of the following methods:

- **salary basis:** a multiple of the key person's current gross annual salary (typically a figure of five- to 10-times salary is used); or
- **profit basis:** up to two-times annual gross profit or up to five-times annual net profit of the business in specific circumstances; or
- **loan basis:** the amount of loans owed by the business, including loans made by the key person to the business.

The tax treatment of proceeds depends on the risk that the insurance covers, i.e. proceeds to cover loss of profits are generally treated as a revenue receipt and are taxed as revenue, whereas proceeds to cover loans are generally treated as a capital receipt and should be exempt from tax.

The costs of key person cover are generally not allowable for tax relief; however, the costs of key person cover to cover loss of profits may be allowable provided specific conditions are met, as below.

Revenue has confirmed that the following four conditions need to be met for key person cover premiums to be admissible deductions for business tax purposes:

1. The relationship between the company and the insured life must be that of employer and employee. (The term 'employee' in this context is taken to include a director.)
2. The employee must have no substantial proprietary interest in the business. (A person is regarded as having a substantial proprietary interest in a company if they own more than 15% of the ordinary share capital.)
3. The life insurance must be intended to meet loss of profit resulting from the loss of the services of the employee as distinct from loss of goodwill or other capital loss. Premiums on policies taken out to cover loans or other outstanding debts that would become repayable on the death of an employee are not admissible deductions.
4. The life policy must be for a fixed short term, usually less than five years, and have no surrender value or investment content.

Appropriate legal and tax advice should be obtained when arranging shareholder cover and/or key person cover, and a financial advisor/broker and the life insurance provider can provide guidance on the setup and ongoing operation of these arrangements.

10 KEY POINTS: LIFE INSURANCE FOR INDIVIDUALS AND BUSINESSES

1. The three main types of life insurance are life cover, income protection/disability cover and specified illness cover.
2. If you have young children, then life cover of 10 to 15 times your gross annual earnings should be considered.
3. The State Illness Income Benefit is approximately €10,000 per annum for a single person; therefore, most working people should consider income protection cover that insures income on an ongoing basis.
4. Employers may provide a level of life insurance benefits for employees. Depending on individual circumstances, employees may need to supplement this cover by personally arranging additional cover.
5. The cost of life cover for self-employed individuals and individuals in 'non-pensionable' employment can be structured so that the cost is allowable for income tax relief in the same manner as personal pension contributions.
6. The cost of life cover and income protection cover for employees can be claimed by employers as a trading expense for business tax purposes.

7. The cost of personal income protection cover that is arranged by an individual is allowable for personal income tax relief at the individual's higher rate of income tax.

8. Specified illness cover is usually available on a stand-alone basis, or in conjunction with life cover. A wide range of illnesses are covered, and a reduced level of cover can apply to some illnesses.

9. The death of a shareholder/partner or a key employee can have significant adverse implications for a business and in some cases can threaten its continued existence. Life insurance for businesses can be structured to insure this risk.

10. Life insurance for businesses consists of shareholder cover and key person cover, and should be structured appropriately, taking into account a number of commercial, tax and legal considerations.

6.

Planning for Retirement

- Introduction
- Assessing What will be Needed in Retirement
- Options for Accessing Retirement Benefits from Pension Plans
- Normal Retirement Age and Early Retirement
- Purchasing an Annuity
- Standard Fund Threshold and Pension Benefit Crystallisation Events
- Approved Retirement Funds (ARFs) and Approved Minimum Retirement Funds (AMRFs)
- Annuity Option vs ARF Option

Introduction

Retirement is a major personal and financial life event. The time many of us will spend in retirement will likely be at least half the time we spend working (assuming we work from our early 20s and retire in our mid-60s). As discussed in the Introduction to this book, just because we stop earning does not mean we stop incurring living costs.

This chapter provides guidance on assessing what individuals need to do to plan for their retirement, focusing on the main options for accessing retirement benefits from defined contribution (DC) pension plans, i.e. pension plans that provide retirement benefits based on an accumulated fund value.

The following topics are covered in this chapter:

* assessing what will be needed in retirement;
* options for accessing retirement benefits from pension plans;
* normal retirement age and early retirement;
* purchasing an annuity;
* standard fund threshold and pension benefit crystallisation events;
* approved retirement funds (ARFs) and approved minimum retirement funds (AMRFs);
* annuity option vs ARF option.

Assessing What will be Needed in Retirement

The key to a financially secure retirement is having enough regular income to meet ongoing living costs. So, how much money will be needed in retirement? In order to calculate how much an individual will need in retirement, a review of current and future costs and expenses, existing and future assets, liabilities, and sources and levels of income should be undertaken. **Figure 6.1** shows the steps to take in doing so.

FIGURE 6.1: STEPS TO ASSESS RETIREMENT NEEDS

Step 1: Review current living expenses.	• Use the checklist in **Figure 6.2** below to estimate current living expenses. • Add extra for additional expenses, e.g. medical costs, extra holidays, more travel, etc.
Step 2: Review current financial costs (e.g. loan repayments and life insurance costs).	• Consider a debt-management strategy to clear debts in a structured and affordable manner. (Ideally, aim to be debt-free by the time of retirement.)

	• Consider whether life insurance will be required in retirement (note: life insurance may be required for any remaining loans or for inheritance tax purposes).
Step 3: Estimate future living costs and future financial costs.	• Calculate the future equivalent of living and financial costs by: – Selecting a preferred retirement date. – Allowing for inflation (of, say, 2% per year) in order to estimate the future equivalent of living and financial costs at the preferred retirement date.
Step 4: List and review: • existing assets; • existing liabilities; • likely sources of income in retirement.	• Include savings and investments, private/public sector pension plans, entitlements to the State pension, etc. • Existing liabilities may include mortgages and other loans.
Step 5: Estimate: • future assets; • future liabilities; and • likely levels of income at the preferred retirement date.	Consider the following: • Applying a prudent rate of growth to existing savings and investments in order to estimate their future values. • Estimating future loan balances, allowing for future interest rate rises, e.g. an increase of 2% or 3% over existing rates. • The level of income that savings and investments can realistically provide at the preferred retirement date and during retirement, e.g. deposit interest on cash deposits, dividend income, rental income, etc. • Entitlement to the State Pension (Contributory) and other state benefits in retirement, including any entitlements for spouse/civil partner/cohabitant. (Contact the Department of Employment Affairs and Social Protection to determine entitlements. In addition, individuals who have worked abroad should check entitlements to a State pension with the relevant countries.) • The likely future values of private/public sector pension plans and the level of income in retirement that these pension plans can realistically provide.

Completing the above steps should provide:

1. a clearer picture of how much will be needed in retirement;
2. an estimate of the future values of assets and liabilities at the preferred retirement date;
3. an estimate of the amount of income that can reasonably be expected from assets and pension plans during retirement.

FIGURE 6.2: LIVING EXPENSES CHECKLIST

	Annual Amount €
Food, drink and household	
Clothing	
Entertainment	
Holidays and travel	
Electricity	
Gas/oil	
Telephone	
TV/digital services/broadband, etc.	
Property maintenance	
Property insurance	
Property tax	
Motor tax and insurance	
Motor fuel and maintenance	
Club subscriptions	
Medical/dental costs	
Health insurance	
Other expenses:	
TOTAL	

Note: expenditure patterns may change during retirement; for example, more may be spent on travel/holidays in the earlier years of retirement, and on medical costs in the later years.

An example of a completed living expenses checklist is shown in **Example 6.1**.

EXAMPLE 6.1: A COMPLETED LIVING EXPENSES CHECKLIST

	Annual Amount
Food, drink and household	€6,000
Clothing	€1,000
Entertainment	€2,000
Holidays and travel	€6,000
Electricity	€1,000
Gas/oil	€1,000
Telephone	€1,000
TV/digital services/broadband, etc.	€1,000
Property maintenance	€1,500
Property insurance	€1,000
Property tax	€1,500
Motor tax and insurance	€1,000
Motor fuel and maintenance	€2,000
Club subscriptions	€2,000
Medical/dental costs	€1,000
Health insurance	€3,500
Other expenses:	€2,000
TOTAL	€34,500

Options for Accessing Retirement Benefits from Pension Plans

A number of options are available for accessing retirement benefits from the accumulated value in a pension plan. The options can consist of a combination of some or all of four options, depending on the type of pension plan, as summarised in **Figure 6.3** below.

FIGURE 6.3: OPTIONS FOR ACCESSING RETIREMENT BENEFITS FROM A PENSION PLAN

Accessing retirement benefits from a pension plan consists of a combination of some or all of the following options:			
1. Purchase an annuity	**2.** Take a lump sum from the pension plan	**3.** Invest in an approved retirement fund (ARF)	**4.** PRSA only: remain invested in a PRSA
Use some or all of the pension plan value to purchase an annuity to provide a secure regular pension income for life.	Under Revenue rules, the maximum allowable lump sum is up to 25% of the pension plan value (or can be based on a multiple of salary for an OPS); some or all of the lump sum can be paid tax-free. The maximum combined tax-free lump sum from all pension plans is €200,000.	Reinvest some/all of capital accumulated in the pension plan in an ARF in order to provide income during retirement, subject to investing €63,500 in an approved minimum retirement fund (AMRF) until age 75, unless specific conditions are met.	In the case of PRSA plans, the remaining value after taking an allowable lump sum, can remain invested in the PRSA (which becomes a 'vested PRSA') with the same treatment that applies to an ARF/AMRF.

In specific circumstances, after taking the initial lump sum as per option 2 above, any remaining balance can be taken as a taxable lump sum.

The availability of the above options depends on the type of pension plan held at retirement, as discussed in the sections below.

Note: the value of pension plan benefits that exceed a specific threshold will be subject to an additional tax charge, as discussed in the section on "Standard Fund Threshold and Pension Benefit Crystallisation Events" later in this chapter.

Normal Retirement Age and Early Retirement

Under Revenue rules, an approved pension plan must have a specified normal retirement age (NRA). Early retirement options are also available in specific circumstances. The NRAs for pension plans and the availability of early retirement options depend on the type of pension plan, as summarised in **Figure 6.4**:

FIGURE 6.4: NRAs AND EARLY RETIREMENT/EARLY ACCESS

Pension Plan Type	NRA	Early Retirement/Early Access
Occupational Pension Scheme (OPS) – see **Chapters 3** and **4**	Between 60 and 70	Age 50 to 60 with trustee consent
Personal Retirement Bond (PRB) – see **Chapter 4**	Between 60 and 70	Age 50 to 60
AVC PRSA (linked to a main OPS) – see **Chapter 4**	Benefits must be taken at the same time as the benefits from the main OPS	Benefits must be taken at the same time as the benefits from the main OPS
PRSA (employee) – see **Chapter 4**	Between 60 and 75	Age 50 to 60
PRSA (self-employed) – see **Chapter 3**	Between 60 and 75	Only on grounds of ill-health
Personal Pension Plan – see **Chapter 3**	Between 60 and 75	Only on grounds of ill-health

Purchasing an Annuity

An annuity is a contract with an insurance company, whereby in exchange for a lump sum payment from a pension plan, the insurance company will pay a regular ongoing income to the pension plan holder for the rest of their life.

The annuity retirement option is available for all types of DC pension plans.

An annuity is purchased by using some or all of the accumulated value in a pension plan (this can be any pension plan, not just an OPS) at retirement, or by using some or all of the accumulated value in an ARF and/or an AMRF during retirement, for example an individual may invest in an ARF/AMRF and then decide at a later date to use an amount in the ARF/AMRF to purchase an annuity.

The amount of income payable depends on available annuity rates at the time of purchasing the annuity, which are based on:

- **age**: annuity rates are generally higher (i.e. provide more income), the older a person is when the annuity is being purchased;
- **interest rates** and **bond yields**: low interest rates and low bond yields typically result in low annuity rates, and vice versa;
- the specific annuity **options** selected (see the section on "Annuity Options" below).

EXAMPLE 6.2: PURCHASING AN ANNUITY

Joe is retiring and has €400,000 in his pension plan. Joe opts to take a 25% lump sum of €100,000 from the pension plan and to use the balance of €300,000 to purchase an annuity from an insurance company.

The applicable annuity rate for Joe is 4% (based on the current available annuity rates), which will provide Joe with a regular income of €12,000 per year, payable as a regular income payment of €1,000 per month for the remainder of his life.

This annual income amount is calculated as the balance in Joe's pension plan of €300,000 × the applicable annuity rate of 4% = €12,000 and is subject to income taxes as applicable.

This annuity income payable to Joe is **in addition to** Joe's entitlement to the State Pension (Contributory).

Annuity Options

A number of options are available when purchasing an annuity. The appropriate options for an individual will depend on the individual's circumstances and preferences, such as the individual's income needs in retirement, other financial assets/savings, etc. The specific options will impact on the annuity rate: some options will result in a higher rate (i.e. a higher level of income) and some options will result in a lower rate (i.e. a lower level of income). The main options are listed below.

- **Standard or enhanced annuity** A standard annuity does not take account of health circumstances. An enhanced annuity does take account of health circumstances and may result in a higher rate (i.e. a higher level of income) than a standard annuity. For example, conditions such as a history of smoking, obesity, diabetes, high blood pressure, heart problems, cancer, etc., may result in the availability of an enhanced annuity, which would pay a higher ongoing income compared to a standard annuity. The reason for a higher level of income is that statistically the underlying medical condition(s) will reduce the individual's life expectancy, and therefore will reduce the annuity payment period, compared to an individual who does not have the underlying medical condition(s).

- **Single or joint life annuities** A single life annuity provides a pension income to an individual during the rest of their life, or up to the end of a 'guaranteed payment period', if applicable (see below). With a single life annuity, no pension is payable to a spouse/registered civil partner/dependant after the individual's death and after the end of the guaranteed payment period (if applicable), i.e. all annuity payments cease and no further benefits are provided.

  With a joint life annuity, a pension income 'reverts to' (i.e. continues to be payable to) a spouse/registered civil partner/dependant after the individual's death. Different 'reversion' rates of spouse/registered civil partner/dependant pension can be selected, e.g. reversion rates of 100%, two-thirds or 50% of the pension income payable to the spouse/registered civil partner/dependant. A single life annuity provides a higher level of income compared to a joint life annuity. Joint life annuities with lower income-reversion rates provide a higher level of income compared to joint life annuities with higher income-reversion rates.

- **Minimum/guaranteed payment period** A minimum, or guaranteed, payment period can be selected when purchasing an annuity, whereby the pension income will be payable for the entire minimum payment period, even if the individual dies before the end of the period. Minimum payment periods are typically five or 10 years. An annuity with a minimum payment period provides a lower level of income compared to an annuity without a minimum payment period.

- **Escalation rate** The income payable can remain fixed and unchanged, or an annual 'escalation rate' can be selected whereby the income will increase each year by that rate (with the objective of providing protection against the impact of inflation). Typical annual escalation rates range between 1 and 5%. An annuity with an escalation rate provides a lower level of income at commencement compared to an annuity without an escalation rate, and the higher the escalation rate the lower the level of income at commencement.

- **Frequency of payment** Pension income can be paid monthly, quarterly, half-yearly or yearly, and can be paid in advance (e.g. at the beginning of the month) or arrears (e.g. at the end of the month).

- **Overlap** For a joint life annuity that features a minimum-payment period, upon the death of the main annuity holder, an annuity with 'overlap' will immediately commence paying the second annuity to the surviving life and, in addition, will continue to pay the main annuity to the second life up to the expiry of the minimum payment period. Therefore, the surviving life would effectively receive **two** income payments up to the expiry of the minimum payment period (i.e. the income amount that had been paid to the annuity holder who has deceased + the income amount payable under the applicable reversion rate, e.g. 100%, two-thirds, 50%, etc.), and thereafter would receive one income payment as per the reversion rate.

Annuity Payments on the Death of the Annuity Holder

On the death of the annuity holder, the annuity income may cease or may continue, depending on the specific options selected, as outlined above. **Figure 6.5** below lists the treatment on death for different annuity types/options.

FIGURE 6.5: ANNUITY PAYMENTS ON DEATH

Type of annuity (annuity options)	Treatment on death
Single life, without minimum payment period	The annuity ceases.
Single life, with minimum payment period	The annuity is payable to the estate/beneficiaries for at least the duration of the minimum payment period and thereafter ceases.
Joint life, without minimum payment period, 50% reversion, no overlap*	50% of the annuity continues to be paid with the same frequency (monthly/quarterly, etc.) to the second life for their lifetime and ceases on the death of the second life.
Joint life, with minimum payment period, 50% reversion, with overlap*	The main annuity is payable for at least the duration of the minimum payment period. 50% of the annuity is payable to the second life from the date of death of the main annuity holder, even if this occurs within the minimum payment period. The second annuity ceases on the second death.

Joint life/with minimum payment period/50% reversion/no overlap*	The main annuity is payable for at least the duration of the minimum payment period. 50% of the annuity is payable to the second life upon the death of the main annuity holder but will only commence at the end of the minimum payment period, when the main annuity payment ceases. The second annuity ceases on the second death.

Source: Irish Life, *All About Annuities* (with permission from Irish Life)
* These examples assume that the second life does not pre-decease the main annuity holder. If the second life pre-deceases the main annuity holder, the annuity income payments cease on the death of the main annuity holder or cease at the end of the minimum payment period, if applicable.

Income payable from an annuity is subject to personal taxes on income in the normal manner, i.e. income tax at the standard or marginal rates, and USC (reduced rates of USC can apply depending on age and income level). Income payable from an annuity is not subject to PRSI.

Once an annuity is purchased, the terms of the annuity cannot be altered and an annuity cannot be subsequently exchanged for a capital value.

Opting for or deciding between an annuity and an ARF is discussed later on in this chapter.

Lump Sum Options

At retirement, many individuals opt to take a lump sum from the accumulated value in their pension plan. Under Revenue rules, the maximum lump sum amount is 25% of the value in the pension plan (see below for guidance on the tax treatment of lump sums).

Individuals with benefits in an OPS also have the option of taking a maximum lump sum based on salary and years of service, as an alternative to the 25% lump sum option. This 'salary/service' based option may be a preferable option, depending on the value of the pension plan and salary levels, as the maximum lump sum may be higher than 25% of the pension plan value. However, if this option is chosen, the balance (if any) in the pension plan after taking the lump sum must be used to purchase an annuity, i.e. the ARF/AMRF option is not available under this option, unless the balance is in respect of AVCs paid by the individual. AVC values can be invested in an ARF/AMRF, if required, under this option.

Under the salary/service option, the maximum lump sum is based on 3/80ths of final salary for each year of service with the employer, up to a maximum of 40 years of service. The maximum lump sum is therefore 120/80ths or 1.5 times final salary for 20+ years of service.

An example of both options is contained in **Example 6.3** below.

Example 6.3: Taking a Lump Sum from an OPS

Karen is retiring at age 65, has a final salary of €50,000 and has 20 years of service with her employer. Karen's pension plan value in the employer-provided OPS is €200,000. The NRA for the OPS is age 65. Karen has not paid AVCs and has no other pension plan entitlements, apart from the State Pension (Contributory).

Karen's options for taking retirement benefits from the OPS are as follows:

Option 1 – 25% option, i.e. a lump sum up to 25% of the pension plan value:

- Karen can opt for a 25% lump sum of €50,000, i.e. pension plan value of €200,000 × 25% = €50,000; and
- Karen can use the balance to purchase an annuity and/or invest in retirement funds (i.e. an ARF/AMRF).

Option 2 – salary/service option, i.e. a lump sum based on salary and years of service:

- Karen can opt for a lump sum based on salary and years of service.
- Karen has at least 20 years of service and therefore can opt for the maximum lump sum of 1.5 times final salary.
- The lump sum is calculated at 1.5 × final salary of €50,000 = lump sum of €75,000.
- Under this option, Karen **must** use the balance of €125,000 to purchase an annuity, i.e. using the balance to invest in retirement funds (ARF/AMRF) is **not** an option.

Under the salary/service option, if an individual has completed more than eight years' service with the employer at normal retirement age, an 'uplifted scale' can be used to calculate the maximum lump sum, as per the table in **Figure 6.6**.

Figure 6.6: Uplifted Scale for Salary/service Lump Sum Calculation

Where the uplifted scale is used the maximum lump sum allowed is the lower of:
- the lump sum entitlement on the "uplifted scale"; or
- 1.5 times final salary, less retained lump sum benefits.

Years of service to NRA	1–8	9	10	11	12	13	14
Maximum lump sum as a fraction of final salary	3/80 p.a.	30/80	36/80	42/80	48/80	54/80	63/80

Years of service to NRA	15	16	17	18	19	20 or more
Maximum lump sum as a fraction of final salary	72/80	81/80	90/80	99/80	108/80	120/80

Source: New Ireland, *Pensions Technical Manual*, p. 17 (with permission from New Ireland)

Fractions of a year can be taken into account; for example, an individual who has completed 14 years and four months service at NRA may be entitled to take 66/80ths of final salary as a lump sum under the salary/service options.

Calculating Maximum Lump Sums on Early Retirement

On early retirement from age 50 onwards, the lump sum options are:

1. 25% option: lump sum up to 25% of the pension plan value;

or

2. salary/service option: lump sum based on salary and years of service.

Under the salary/service option, the maximum lump sum is the **higher** of:

(a) 3/80ths of final salary for each year of actual service;

or

(b) the following calculation:

$$\frac{\text{actual years of service at early retirement age}}{\text{potential years of service to NRA}} \times \frac{\text{maximum lump}}{\text{sum at NRA}}$$

In (b) above, lump sum(s) due on retirement from any other pension plan(s) must be deducted from the maximum lump sum at NRA.

If the individual has completed **less than 20 years' service**, the maximum benefits at (b) above cannot exceed the maximum lump sum the individual would have received, assuming that actual service ended at NRA. This restriction means that the lump sum calculated using (b) above must be restricted to the lump sum entitlement under the uplifted scale, based on actual completed service.

An example of the salary/service lump sum calculation on early retirement is contained in **Example 6.4** below.

EXAMPLE 6.4: SALARY/SERVICE LUMP SUM CALCULATION ON EARLY RETIREMENT

The NRA for an employer-provided OPS is age 65. Two members in the OPS, Lara and Susan, are taking early retirement at age 58 under the salary/service option. Lara and Susan do not have any other pension plan benefits. Both have a final salary of €50,000; Lara has completed 20 years of service and Susan has completed 10 years of service.

Lara:

Lara's maximum lump sum on early retirement is the **higher** of:

(a) **20 actual years × 3/80ths per year × €50,000 final salary = a lump sum of €37,500;**

or

(b) **20 actual years / 27 potential years × 'maximum lump sum at NRA'.**

Lara's 'maximum lump sum at NRA' in the formula at (b) above, as per the Uplifted Scale (see **Figure 6.6**), is 120/80 × €50,000 = €75,000.

So, 20 actual years / 27 potential years × €75,000 = a lump sum €55,555.

The maximum lump sum available to Lara on early retirement is the higher of the above calculations, i.e. €55,555.

Susan:

Susan's maximum lump sum on early retirement is the **higher** of:

(a) 10 actual years × 3/80ths per year × €50,000 final salary = a lump sum of €18,750;

or

(b) 10 actual years / 17 potential year × 'maximum lump sum at NRA'.

Susan's 'maximum potential lump sum at NRA' in the formula at (b), as per the Uplifted Scale (see **Figure 6.6**), is 90/80 × €50,000 = €56,250.

So, 10 actual years / 17 potential years × €56,250 = €33,088

However, as Susan has completed less than 20 years' service, option (b) cannot exceed the retirement lump sum entitlement based on actual service on the uplifted scale, which is calculated at 36/80 × €50,000 = €22,500.

Therefore, the maximum lump sum available to Susan on early retirement is €22,500, under the salary/service option.

Note: Under the salary/service lump sum option, the balance (if any) in the main OPS after taking a lump sum must be used to purchase an annuity, and the value of any AVC funds can also be used to purchase an annuity or can be invested in an ARF/AMRF.

Tax Treatment of Lump Sums

The tax treatment of lump sums is as follows:

- the cumulative maximum tax-free lump sum from all pension plans is €200,000;
- the portion of any lump sum amount between €200,000 and €500,000 is subject to tax at the standard rate (currently 20%);

- the portion of any lump sum amount above €500,000 is subject to tax at the higher rate (currently 40%) and USC, and PRSI if applicable.

These limits apply to all lump sums paid since 7 December 2005. The applicable tax is deducted at source by the pension plan provider.

Standard Fund Threshold and Pension Benefit Crystallisation Events

The combined capital value of all benefits accrued in pension plans for an individual is subject to a lifetime limit or threshold, known as the standard fund threshold (SFT), whereby the capital value of pension benefits that exceeds the SFT is subject to an additional tax charge. This threshold applies to all individuals (i.e. employees, company owners, self-employed individuals).

The current SFT is €2 million. The SFT was first introduced with effect from 7 December 2005. A higher threshold called the personal fund threshold (PFT) may apply in the following circumstances:

- where an individual had a capital value of pension rights greater than €5 million on 7 December 2005; or
- greater than €2.3 million on 7 December 2010; or
- greater than €2 million on 1 January 2014; and
- provided specific Revenue notification requirements were met; then
- that individual can have a personal fund threshold (PFT) based on the value of their pension rights and the pre-existing SFT (if any) on those dates. Any PFT granted replaces the SFT for these individuals.

In the event that pension benefits exceed the SFT (or PFT), the excess, known as a 'chargeable excess', is subject to income tax at the higher rate (currently 40%), which is paid directly from the pension plan by the pension plan administrator. The tax is triggered following a 'benefit crystallisation event' (BCE).

If standard rate income tax has been paid on the retirement lump sum (which is very likely to be the case), the tax deducted from the retirement lump sum can be used to offset the tax due on any excess over the SFT – see **Example 6.5** below.

EXAMPLE 6.5: CALCULATING THE TAX PAYABLE ON A 'CHARGEABLE EXCESS'

Seán is aged 60 and has a pension plan valued at €2,200,000. He wishes to access retirement benefits from the pension plan as follows:
- withdraw a lump sum of €500,000 (which is less than the 25% lump sum limit, as any lump sum amount above €500,000 would be subject to tax at the higher rate, currently 40%, and USC and PRSI – Seán has decided to take €500,000 as the lump sum in order to avoid these higher taxes);
- invest the balance in retirement funds (i.e. an ARF and an AMRF).

Seán does not have any other pension plans in place and has not previously accessed retirement benefits from pension plans.

Step 1 – calculate the tax on the lump sum

Lump sum	€500,000
Less tax-free amount	-€200,000
Balance subject to tax at the standard rate	€300,000
Tax at 20%	€60,000

Step 2 – calculate the tax on the chargeable excess

Pension plan value	€2,200,000
Less SFT	-€2,000,000
Chargeable excess	€200,000
Tax at 40%	€80,000
Less standard rate tax deducted from lump sum as per Step 1	-€60,000
Tax on the chargeable excess	€20,000

Summary

Lump sum to be withdrawn by Seán	€500,000
Less tax as per Step 1	-€60,000
Net lump sum payable to Seán	€440,000
Balance of pension plan to be transferred to ARF/AMRF	€1,700,000
Less tax on the chargeable excess as per Step 2	-€20,000
Net amount to be transferred to ARF/AMRF	€1,680,000

A BCE is an event occurring on or after 7 December 2005 (i.e. the date from which the SFT was introduced), where an individual becomes entitled to receive a benefit from a pension plan. In the example above, Seán's decision to access his retirement benefits is a BCE.

An individual's SFT (or PFT) is reduced/eliminated by the value of the pension benefit arising on a BCE, i.e. the threshold is reduced over time if the individual takes pension benefits at different times.

A BCE occurs when an individual takes any of the following:

- a retirement lump sum;
- an annuity;
- an ARF option;
- for defined benefits plans and public sector plans, an increase of a pension in payment in excess of the greater of 5% p.a. or CPI plus 2%, i.e. an increase to regular pension income being paid that is greater than this limit. This limit is an anti-tax avoidance measure to prevent commencement of a pension at a low rate in order to bring the capitalised value of the pension benefit below the SFT, with the pension subsequently increased at an accelerated rate after the benefit has been valued for BCE purposes;
- a transfer to an overseas pension scheme.

Approved Retirement Funds (ARFs) and Approved Minimum Retirement Funds (AMRFs)

The value in a pension plan on retirement (or the balance in a pension plan, after withdrawing a lump sum based on up to 25% of the pension plan value), can be invested in an ARF as an alternative to purchasing an annuity. As mentioned in **Figure 6.3** above, in the case of PRSA plans, the remaining value after taking an allowable lump sum, can remain invested in the PRSA (which becomes a 'vested PRSA') with the same treatment that applies to an ARF/AMRF, as set out below:

- An ARF is a post-retirement planning investment and drawdown vehicle that provides the flexibility of beneficial ownership of the capital invested in the fund, with a wide range of investment options.
- The funds invested in an ARF are used to provide an income to the ARF holder.
- For income tax purposes, at least 4% of the value of an ARF is **deemed to be withdrawn** by the ARF holder each year from the commencement of the ARF, or the year they become age 61, whichever is later, i.e. income taxes are due by the ARF holder on the 4% withdrawal amount, whether or not the withdrawal is actually made. This '**minimum deemed withdrawal**' increases to 5% in the year the ARF holder becomes 71.
- If the total combined value of ARFs and vested PRSAs exceed €2 million in value, at least 6% of the value of the ARFs and vested PRSAs is deemed to be withdrawn each year for income tax purposes from the commencement of the ARF, or the year the ARF holder becomes age 61, whichever is later.
- More than 4% of the value can be withdrawn from an ARF each year as an income if required, i.e. no maximum withdrawal limit applies.
- An amount of €63,500 must be invested in an AMRF, unless guaranteed pension income of at least €12,700 per annum exists (e.g. State pension income).
- An AMRF becomes an ARF:
  - when the individual is aged 75; or
  - when the individual dies; or
  - if the individual subsequently starts to receive pension income of at least €12,700 per annum.

- A single income withdrawal of 4% per year is permitted from an AMRF. (*Note*: this withdrawal is **optional** and income taxes are not due if the withdrawal is not made, unlike the deemed withdrawal requirement for an ARF – see above). A higher withdrawal from an

AMRF cannot be made, i.e. the only withdrawal option is 4% per year as a single withdrawal.

- All withdrawals from an ARF and an AMRF are treated as income for personal tax purposes, i.e. subject to income tax at the standard or marginal rates as applicable, USC and PRSI, if applicable.
- The value in an ARF and/or an AMRF can be used to purchase an annuity at any stage.
- Original capital invested in an ARF/AMRF is not guaranteed (unless explicit capital security is provided by the investments held in the ARF/AMRF), and values can fall as well as rise in value.
- Income withdrawals plus annual ARF/AMRF charges may exceed the growth (if any) of the investments within an ARF/AMRF and accordingly the value of an ARF/AMRF may be reduced or eliminated over time before the holder dies, even if the investments rise in value (this is known as 'bomb-out' risk).
- The treatment of an ARF/AMRF on death of the holder is summarised in **Figure 6.7** below.

FIGURE 6.7: ARF/AMRF TREATMENT ON DEATH

ARF/AMRF inherited by	Income Tax due?	Capital Acquisitions Tax due?
Surviving spouse or registered civil partner.	None, if transferred into an ARF in the spouse or registered civil partner's name. Income taxes payable on any future withdrawals.	No.
Children aged 21 and over.	Yes, at a rate of 30%.	No.
Children under age 21.	None.	Yes, subject to exemption limits that apply for inheritances from parents.
Others (including surviving spouse or registered civil partner if value of the ARF/AMRF is paid out as a lump sum).	Yes, at deceased's income tax rate at the time of death (either 20% or 40% at present).	Yes, subject to exemption limits that apply for inheritances. No CAT on inheritances taken from spouses or civil partners.

Example 6.6 below contains a graphical example of opting for a 25% lump sum and ARF/AMRF.

EXAMPLE 6.6: OPTING FOR AN **ARF/AMRF**

Mary has a defined contribution pension plan value of €300,000 and wishes to access retirement benefits from the pension fund by taking 25% of the value of the fund as a lump sum and investing the balance in an ARF/AMRF. Mary has no other pension entitlements, apart from the State Pension (Contributory).

Mary's lump sum and ARF/AMRF options are as follows:

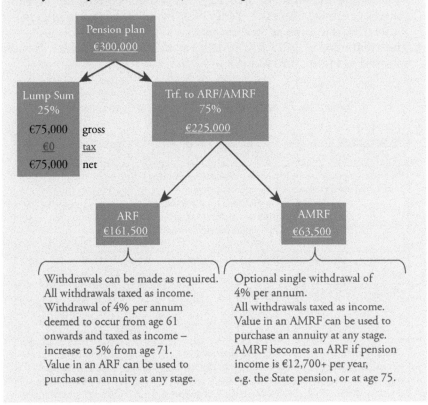

ARF €161,500	AMRF €63,500
Withdrawals can be made as required. All withdrawals taxed as income. Withdrawal of 4% per annum deemed to occur from age 61 onwards and taxed as income – increase to 5% from age 71. Value in an ARF can be used to purchase an annuity at any stage.	Optional single withdrawal of 4% per annum. All withdrawals taxed as income. Value in an AMRF can be used to purchase an annuity at any stage. AMRF becomes an ARF if pension income is €12,700+ per year, e.g. the State pension, or at age 75.

Annuity Option vs ARF Option

The decision to purchase an annuity or invest in an ARF/AMRF depends on a number of factors, including:

- **Personal circumstances** This includes income requirements in retirement, number of dependants (if any), other assets and liabilities at retirement, other income sources, and the level of outgoings in retirement.
- **Age** Annuity rates are lower for younger individuals purchasing an annuity, i.e. the annuity income levels are lower compared to annuity income levels for older individuals purchasing an annuity. If an ARF/AMRF is being considered, the individual needs to be aware that income withdrawals over a longer period may reduce and possibly deplete in full the ARF/AMRF, i.e. the entire value in the ARF/AMRF could be spent before the individual dies. This risk is potentially greater for younger ARF/AMRF holders. (For example, the risk of the entire value of the ARF/AMRF being spent before an individual dies is potentially greater for a 60-year-old individual commencing an ARF/AMRF, compared to a 70-year-old individual commencing an ARF/AMRF.)
- **Security and predictability** An annuity provides a secure and predictable regular level of income for life that is known at the outset. The annuity provider pays the income on an ongoing basis in accordance with the terms of the annuity. Once an annuity is purchased, the individual recipient of the annuity income does not need to make investment decisions or consider further options regarding this income. In contrast, an ARF/AMRF is an investment fund that can contain investments that can fall as well as rise in value; thus, the level of income is not secure and predictable at the outset, and the value of the ARF/AMRF could be depleted in full before the individual dies.
- **Flexibility** Once an annuity is purchased, the terms cannot be altered or reversed. An ARF/AMRF provides more flexibility in that the individual retains beneficial ownership of the investment capital and can decide on and change the amount of income to be withdrawn (subject to the minimum deemed withdrawal requirements, and the risk of the ARF/AMRF being spent before the individual dies, as discussed above). In addition, an ARF/AMRF holder has the option of using some or all of the ARF/AMRF value to purchase an annuity at any stage in the future, if required.
- **Market conditions** Low interest rates and low bond yields result in low annuity rates and thus low annuity income levels, which have prevailed in recent years; however, rising interest rates and higher bond yields should result in higher annuity rates and thus higher annuity income levels.

10 Key Points: Planning for Retirement

1. Retirement is a major personal and financial life event, and advance planning is very important.
2. The time many of us will spend in retirement will likely be at least half the time we spend working.
3. Assessing current and future living expenses, and existing and future assets, liabilities and sources and levels of income will help individuals to calculate how much they will need in retirement.
4. Depending on the pension plan, to access benefits from the plan, an individual can: purchase an annuity; take a lump sum; invest in a retirement fund (ARF/AMRF), and/or remain invested in a PRSA (PRSA only).
5. An annuity providing a secure regular pension income for life is available for all types of defined contribution pension plans. A number of options are available when purchasing an annuity.
6. Individuals with benefits in an occupational pension scheme also have the option of taking a lump sum based on salary and years of service (up to 1.5 times pensionable salary for 20+ years of service).
7. The maximum tax-free lump sum from all pension plans is €200,000.
8. The combined capital value of all benefits accrued in pension plans is subject to a lifetime limit or threshold, known as the standard fund threshold (SFT), whereby the capital value of pension benefits that exceeds the SFT is subject to an additional tax charge.
9. An ARF/AMRF is a post-retirement planning investment and drawdown vehicle that provides the flexibility of beneficial ownership of the capital invested in the fund, with a wide range of investment options. The funds invested in an ARF/AMRF are used to provide an income to the ARF/AMRF holder.
10. On death, any remaining value in an ARF/AMRF can pass to the surviving spouse or registered civil partner, to children or to anyone else as provided for through the will of the deceased ARF/AMRF holder.

7.

Separation and Divorce

- Introduction
- Pension Adjustment Orders
- Retirement Benefits Orders
- Earmarking and Pension Splitting
- Transfer Out Without Non-member's Consent
- Contingent Benefits Order
- Nominal Value PAO
- Impact of a PAO on Limits for Retirement and Death Benefits

Introduction

Pension plan benefits are usually included in a separation/divorce agreement regarding the division of assets between the separating persons. Two routes are typically available:

1. Pension plan benefits are taken into account in a separation/divorce agreement in dividing other assets, such as property, savings, etc. (For example, Spouse A retains the full value of their pension plan and Spouse B retains the full value of a joint savings account.)
2. Pension plan benefits are formally divided by a court order known as a 'pension adjustment order' (PAO). As pension plan benefits are generally non-assignable, the only valid way to transfer a person's rights under a pension plan to another person is by a PAO.

The following areas are covered in this chapter:

- pension adjustment orders (PAOs);
- retirement benefits orders (i.e. a PAO for a pension plan benefit);
- earmarking and pension splitting;
- transfer out without non-member's consent;
- contingent benefits orders (i.e. a PAO for a death-in-service benefit);
- nominal value PAOs;
- impact of a PAO on limits for retirement and death benefits.

Note: this chapter provides a general overview only of pension plans in the context of separation and divorce. Appropriate legal advice should always be obtained when dealing with matters in this area.

Pension Adjustment Orders

A pension adjustment order (PAO) is a court order to divide pension plan benefits that can be granted in respect of:

- a **retirement benefit**, i.e. pension plan benefits available on retirement; and/or
- a **contingent benefit**, i.e. benefits payable on death-in-service.

PAOs were introduced by the Family Law Act 1995 and the Family Law (Divorce) Act 1996. Prior to these Acts, the division of pension plan benefits in a separation agreement was not legally enforceable.

The Civil Partnership and Certain Rights and Obligations of Cohabitants Act 2010 further provided:

(a) for persons who are in a registered civil partnership to be treated the same as married couples in terms of the ability to seek and obtain PAOs;

(b) that in the case of qualified cohabitants, either cohabitant may apply for a PAO in respect of retirement benefits and contingent benefits at the end of the relationship.

The 2010 Act defines a 'qualified cohabitant' as:

> "an adult who was in a relationship of cohabitation with another adult and who, immediately before the time that that relationship ended, whether through death or otherwise, was living with the other adult as a couple for a period (a) of 2 years or more, in the case where they are the parents of one or more dependent children, and (b) of 5 years or more, in any other case."

However, the 2010 Act does not provide for a PAO in favour of the dependent child of cohabitants. Furthermore, under this Act, qualified cohabitants can contract out of their right to apply for a PAO by entering into a cohabitation agreement, which is a written agreement between parties who have chosen to live together in an intimate and committed relationship, and who are not married to each other and not in a registered civil partnership.

A PAO can be made for benefits in the following pension arrangements:

- occupational pension schemes (OPSs);
- additional voluntary contribution (AVC) plans;
- personal retirement bonds/buy-out bonds;
- personal retirement savings accounts (PRSAs);
- personal pension plans/retirement annuity contracts (RACs);
- trust RACs;
- annuities.

Please note that **separate** PAOs are required for retirement benefits and contingent benefits in an OPS, and separate PAOs are required for each individual private pension arrangement held by each spouse/civil partner/qualified cohabitant.

Retirement funds (i.e. ARFs/AMRFs) are not specifically mentioned in the relevant legislation; however, a different type of court order called a 'property adjustment order' can issue in respect of ARF/AMRF benefits.

A PAO is issued by the court to the trustee of the pension arrangement. For the purposes of a PAO, a 'trustee' can be deemed to be the following:

FIGURE 7.1: DEEMED TRUSTEES FOR A PAO

Pension Arrangement/Trust	Deemed Trustee
OPSs/Trust RACs	The trustee(s) of the plan
Personal retirement bonds/buy-out bonds	The provider, such as a life insurance company
Personal pension plans/individual RACs	The life insurance company provider
PRSAs	The provider, such as a life insurance company
Civil and public service pension schemes	Government department or state agency pension administrators
Annuities	The life insurance company provider

Retirement Benefits Orders

'Retirement benefits' refer to all benefits payable to the member of a pension plan and include retirement pension income, retirement lump sums, benefits payable following the member's death in retirement, and periodic increases on pensions in payment.

This type of PAO will designate a proportion of the member's pension plan benefit for payment to the 'non-member', i.e. the other spouse/registered civil partner/qualified cohabitant that is not a member of the pension plan and in whose favour the PAO is granted, or a dependent child of the member spouse – referred to as the 'designated benefit'.

The designated benefit must specify the following:

- the relevant period, i.e. the period over which retirement benefits, that are to be made subject to the PAO, were earned. While there is flexibility regarding the start of the relevant period, it must end no later than the date of the granting of the relevant decree; and
- the relevant percentage, i.e. the proportion of the retirement benefits earned during the relevant period that is to be allocated to the person specified in the PAO.

Accordingly, the PAO made by the court must specify a relevant period over which the designated benefit is deemed to have accrued together with a relevant percentage.

A PAO for a retirement benefit can be sought at any time on or after the relevant decree, provided that the non-member seeking the order has not remarried or entered into a new registered civil partnership or, in the case of a person representing a dependent child, that the child is still a dependant.

A 'dependent child' is a child who:

- is under the age of 18; or
- is under the age of 23 and in full-time education; or
- has a mental or physical disability, regardless of age.

Example 7.1 below contains an example of how a designated benefit is calculated.

EXAMPLE 7.1: DESIGNATED BENEFIT CALCULATION

Liam joined his employer's OPS in 1998. He married on 1 January 2000, but subsequently separated five years later.

On 1 January 2010, Liam was granted a decree of divorce and a PAO for retirement benefits was made in favour of his spouse, Laura. The PAO specified:

- the relevant period: from 1 January 2000 to 1 January 2010 (10 years); and
- the relevant percentage: 50%.

The contributions paid into the OPS during the relevant period amounted to €50,000.

When Liam retired on 1 January 2015, the value of these contributions in the OPS was €80,000.

Accordingly, the value of the designated benefit for the non-member spouse (i.e. Laura) at the date of Liam's retirement was: €80,000 × 50% = €40,000.

Earmarking and Pension Splitting

When a pension plan benefit has been divided under a PAO, the non-member can either take no action (and the benefit is 'earmarked' to be accessed by the non-member at a later date) or the non-member can decide to formally split the benefit.

- **Earmarking** The non-member takes no action and the designated benefit pays out retirement benefits **at the same time** as retirement benefits start to be paid to the member. As a result, any decision taken by the member to retire earlier or later than their normal retirement age (NRA) will affect the payment of the designated benefit to the non-member. In addition, the non-member will have no control over the investment of the pension assets that have been earmarked for their benefit, and if the trustees allow member fund choice, the future value of the designated benefit will depend on fund(s) selected by the member.
- **Pension Splitting** The relevant percentage of a 'retirement benefit' that has been designated for a non-member is valued and split away from the member's benefit, and is therefore no longer affected by decisions taken by the member. The option to split a benefit is not available if the PAO is made in favour of a dependent child.

The value of the earmarked benefit is calculated as if the member were leaving service on the date of the valuation, and the proportionate value is then allocated to the non-member. Once valued, the earmarked benefit is then transferred to:

- a separate pension account within the same pension plan; or
- another pension plan of which the former spouse/civil partner/ cohabitant is a member; or
- a personal retirement bond, PRSA or a personal pension plan/ retirement annuity contract (RAC) in the name of the former spouse/civil partner/cohabitant, subject to normal transfer rules (though the standard restrictions for transfers from an OPS to a PRSA do not apply).

The non-member can apply at any time after the PAO has been granted to have the retirement benefit split away, provided benefits have not commenced.

Transfer Out Without Non-member's Consent

The trustees of a pension plan can compulsorily transfer a non-member's designated benefit to another plan if:

- the plan is a defined contribution plan;

OR

- the member ceases to be a member of the plan (otherwise than on death);

157

AND IN EACH CASE

- the following conditions apply:
  - the trustees must be satisfied that the charges, fees and costs of the new plan are reasonable;
  - at least 30 days' written notice of the transfer must have been received by the non-member before the transfer is made;
  - no outstanding request exists from the non-member for a transfer payment to another plan;
  - the trustees should confirm to the non-member and to the court that granted the PAO: (a) the amount transferred, and (b) the pension arrangement to which the amount was transferred.

Contingent Benefits Order

A PAO in respect of a contingent benefit refers to benefits payable under the rules of a pension plan in the event of the death of a member during the period of employment to which the plan relates.

'Benefits' include lump sum benefits and pensions payable to dependants. A PAO for contingent benefits ceases once the member leaves the employment to which the plan on which the order has been made relates.

A PAO for a contingent benefit will specify if all or a percentage of the member's benefit is payable on the member's death in service to the non-member or for the benefit of a dependent child.

Nominal Value PAO

The legislation does not allow for a PAO to be made for zero value. As a result, a practice has evolved of a nominal PAO being made where the parties involved in the break-up agree not to seek a share of the other's pension plan benefits.

A nominal value PAO has no commercial value and generally consists of a relevant period of just one day and a relevant percentage of just 0.001%, which means in practice that the PAO value is negligible/nil.

A nominal value PAO will state that it is fixed and not subject to variation. The inclusion of a statement that the PAO cannot be varied is essential if the intention is that the non-member is not to access the member's pension plan benefits.

Impact of a PAO on Limits for Retirement and Death Benefits

As discussed in **Chapter 6**, limits apply to retirement benefits, including:

- the combined capital value of all benefits accrued in pension plans for an individual is subject to a lifetime limit or threshold; and
- the maximum combined tax-free lump sum from all pension plans is €200,000 (payable since 7 December 2005).

Also as discussed in **Chapter 6**:

- the lifetime limit, or threshold, is known as the standard fund threshold (SFT), whereby the capital value of pension benefits that exceeds the SFT is subject to an additional tax charge;
- the current SFT is €2 million and a higher threshold called the personal fund threshold (PFT) may apply in specific circumstances;
- in the event that pension benefits exceed the SFT (or PFT), the excess, known as a 'chargeable excess', is subject to income tax at the higher rate (currently 40%), which should be paid directly from the pension fund by the pension plan administrator;
- the tax is triggered following a 'benefit crystallisation event';
- if standard rate income tax has been paid on the retirement lump sum (which is very likely to be the case), the tax deducted from the retirement lump sum can be used to offset the tax due on any excess over the SFT.

When calculating the capital value of a pension plan member's benefits at retirement for the purposes of the SFT, the designated benefit payable under a PAO at retirement is deemed to be part of the member's retirement benefits. Therefore, the designated benefit is deemed to be a retained benefit even if transferred to another pension arrangement for the non-member.

The designated benefit in the hands of the non-member is not deemed to be a retained benefit for the purposes of the SFT for the non-member.

Any additional tax charge arising on a chargeable excess as a result of a PAO must be apportioned between both parties, i.e. the member and the non-member. This tax liability follows both parties to wherever they transfer their benefits.

Revenue's Pensions Manual contains the following example on the above treatment:

EXAMPLE 7.2: APPORTIONING TAX ARISING ON A CHARGEABLE EXCESS

Eamonn has a PRSA with a value of €1.5 million at the point of crystallisation. He does not have a PFT. A PAO had been made in respect of the PRSA in favour of Eamonn's former spouse, Joan.

At that time, a transfer value of €1 million was paid out of the PRSA in respect of Joan's designated benefit to a separate PRSA with a different PRSA provider.

The capital value of the BCE arising on the crystallisation of Eamonn's PRSA is determined as if no PAO had been made. The PRSA administrator must therefore calculate the investment return earned by the PRSA from the date the transfer value was paid out to Joan's PRSA, to the date of crystallisation of Eamonn's PRSA.

For the purposes of this example we assume a return of 20%, and that the higher rate of income tax at the time of crystallisation is 40%.

The capital value of Eamonn's BCE is therefore deemed to be €1.5 million + (€1m × 120%) = €2.7 million.

This gives rise to a chargeable excess of €0.7 million and chargeable excess tax of €0.28 million (€2.7m − €2m (SFT) = €0.7m; tax @ 40% = €0.28m).

The chargeable excess tax must be divided as follows:

In Joan's case it is: €0.28m × €1m (the actual transfer amount)/€2.7m (the deemed capital value of the BCE) = €103,704.

In Eamonn's case it is: €0.28m × €1.7m (Eamonn's deemed share of the BCE)/€2.7m (the deemed capital value of the BCE) = €176,296.

Source: Revenue Commissioners, *Pensions Manual*, Chapter 25, Limit on Tax Relieved Pension Funds.

The tax-free lump sum entitlement under the terms of the PAO is up to €200,000 for each party, i.e. the member and the non-member. As discussed in **Chapter 6**, any lump sum amount paid over this limit of €200,000 and up to €500,000 is subject to tax at the standard rate (i.e. 20% at present), and any lump sum amount paid over €500,000 is subject to tax at the higher rate (i.e. 40% at present) plus USC, plus PRSI, if applicable.

A death-in-service benefit payable under a PAO is also considered to be the member's death-in-service benefit and will be taken into account for the purpose of Revenue maximum benefits on death in service. For example, as discussed in the section on "Ill-health and Death Benefits from an OPS" in **Chapter 3**, the maximum lump sum payable from an OPS on death prior to retirement is four times final salary, plus an amount equal to the return of the value of the deceased member's own contributions (including AVCs, if any). Any balance in the OPS would then be used to provide a dependant's pension, by purchasing an annuity.

10 KEY POINTS: SEPARATION AND DIVORCE

1. Pension plan benefits are usually included in a separation/ divorce agreement. The division of pension plan benefits is effected by a court order known as a pension adjustment order (PAO).
2. A PAO can be granted in respect of:

   - a retirement benefit, i.e. a pension benefit available on retire-ment; and/or
   - a contingent benefit, i.e. benefits payable on death in service.

3. Separate PAOs are required for retirement benefits and con-tingent benefits in an OPS, and separate PAOs are required for each individual private pension arrangement held by each spouse/civil partner.
4. A PAO in respect of a retirement benefit will designate a pro-portion of the member's pension plan benefit (referred to as the 'designated benefit') for payment to the 'non-member', i.e. the other spouse/registered civil partner/qualified cohabitant that is not a member of the pension plan and in whose favour the PAO is granted, or dependent child of the member spouse.
5. Retirement funds (i.e. ARFs/AMRFs) are not specifically men-tioned in the relevant legislation; however, a different type of court order called a 'property adjustment order' can issue in respect of ARF/AMRF benefits.

6. When a pension plan benefit has been divided under a PAO, the non-member beneficiary can either take no action (and the benefit is 'earmarked' to be accessed by the non-member at a later date) or can decide to formally split the benefit.

7. A 'nominal PAO' can be made where the parties involved in the break-up agree not to seek a share of the other's pension plan benefits.

8. When calculating the capital value of a member's benefits at retirement for the purposes of the SFT, the designated benefit payable under a PAO at retirement is deemed to be part of the member's retirement benefits. The designated benefit in the hands of the non-member is not deemed to be a retained benefit for the purposes of the SFT for the non-member.

9. Any additional tax charge arising on a 'chargeable excess' as a result of a PAO must be apportioned between both parties, i.e. the member and the non-member.

10. The tax-free lump sum entitlement under the terms of the PAO is up to €200,000 for each party, i.e. the member and the non-member.

Index